THE LATIN REAL EASY BOOK

SALSA/AFRO-CUBAN
BRAZILIAN MUSIC
LATIN JAZZ

Including Instructional Material
tailored to fit each tune

Editor and Publisher - Chuck Sher
Musical Editor - Larry Dunlap
Editorial Consultant - Rebeca Mauleón
Music Engraving - Chuck Gee
Cover Design - Jennifer Hewitson and Attila Nagy
Produced by Sher Music Co. in conjunction with
The Stanford Jazz Workshop, www.stanfordjazz.org

©2011 Sher Music Co., P.O. Box 445, Petaluma, CA 94953
www.shermusic.com. No part of this book may be reproduced
in any form without written permission from the publisher.
All Rights Reserved. International Copyright Secured.

ISBN 1-883217-67-9

CATEGORICAL INDEX OF TUNES

(As played and/or written by the following artists)

LATIN JAZZ

CAL TJADER
Fuji
Soul Sauce
Viva Cepeda
Tumbao

PONCHO SANCHEZ
Hey Bud
Ritmo Remo
Sambroso

HORACE SILVER
Señor Blues
Liberated Brother

REBECA MAULEON
No Borders

ANDY NARELL
Chakalaka
We Kinda Music
The Long Way Back

DON GROLNICK
Rojo Y Negro
Heart Of Darkness

PAQUITO D'RIVERA
Chucho

DIZZY GILLESPIE
Tin Tin Deo

RAY OBIEDO
Real Life

RAY BARRETTO
Montuno Blue
On A Sunday Afternoon

PETE ESCOVEDO
Zina's Zamba
Tassajara

MARK LEVINE
Havana
Nana

MANNY OQUENDO
Little Sunflower

VICTOR FELDMAN
Let's Go Dancing

TITO PUENTE
Triton

GEORGE BENSON
My Latin Brother

STEVE SWALLOW
Ladies In Mercedes

HENDRIK MEURKENS
Bolero Para Paquito

ED SMITH
Smooth Samba

MICHAEL P. MOSSMAN
A Song For Horace

SALSA/AFRO-CUBAN

SALSA STANDARDS
Lágrimas Negras
Suavecito
La Mujer de Antonio
Rico Vacilón
Pa' Gozar
De Repente

TITO RODRIGUEZ
Inolvidable
Si Te Contara

EDDIE PALMIERI
La Malanga
Muñeca
Congo Yambumba
Nunca Contigo

LOUIS RAMIREZ
Sabroso Guaguancó

ROBERTO TORRES
Caballo Viejo

MARIO BAUZA
El Marelito
Así No, Papá
Mambo Rincón
Azulito

ORQUESTA ARAGON
Pare Cochero
Tres Lindas Cubanas

PATADO VALDEZ
Opita's Opus

RAY BARRETTO
La Cuna
Guararé

REBECA MAULEON
Rico Cha-Cha-Chá
Yuca Con Mojo

DESCARGA BORICUA
Que Le Den Candela

HECTOR LAVOE
Rompe Saragüey

BRAZILIAN MUSIC

ANTONIO CARLOS JOBIM
Agua de Beber
This Happy Madness
Samba do Aviao
Passarim
Lamento

IVAN LINS
Camaleão
She Walks This Earth
Renata Maria
Jobiniando

DJAVAN
Celeuma
Dia Azul
Asa

**JOÃO DONATO &
GILBERTO GIL**
Lugar Comum
Bananeira

MOACIR SANTOS
Nana

CHICO PINHEIRO
Ao Vento (The Wind)
There's A Storm Inside

BADEN POWELL
Berimbau

RICARDO PEIXOTO
Acrobata

AIRTO
Partido Alto

LARRY DUNLAP
Cafe Rio
Around The Corner

LUIZ BONFA
A Day In The Life Of A Fool

**NELSON FARIA &
GILSON PERANZZETTA**
Rua Bougainville

MAURICIO EINHORN
Estamos Aí

Photo©Chuck Gee

LARRY DUNLAP, IVAN LINS & BOBBE NORRIS

ALPHABETICAL INDEX OF TUNES

PART 1 - Easier Tunes

PART 2 - More Advanced Tunes

A Note From The Publisher

THE FOURTH "REAL EASY BOOK"! - We are thrilled to bring to you this fourth in the series of "Real Easy Books," publications which have been widely-adopted by school systems to help band directors raise the next generation of jazz players. If you aren't familiar with them, please see www.shermusic.com for complete descriptions, songlists, etc. for the earlier volumes. The basic idea of this series of books is to present beginning and/or intermediate-level tunes on one page, and then all the things a band director might have to write out for their students on the page facing each tune—sample piano voicings, bass lines, guitar voicings, scales for soloing, etc. A great idea, road-tested for many years at Stanford Jazz Workshop.

THE IMPORTANCE OF LATIN MUSIC TO JAZZ - One of the great aspects of the world "getting smaller" is that the music of different cultures is now easily accessible by musicians, no matter where they live. Latin music, in particular, has become an integral part of jazz music, and virtually every professional jazz player has some degree of proficiency with Brazilian music, various forms of Afro-Cuban music, and Latin jazz. So in educating the musicians of the future, it is crucial that they have access to accurate charts and good instruction with which to learn these passionate and heartfelt styles of music. To the best of our ability we have provided this in "The Latin Real Easy Book." We hope you have as much fun learning the tunes in this collection as we did in compiling it (and we had a ball!).

PART 1 AND PART 2 SONGS - Besides its value as a classroom text, this book will certainly be used by people who just want more great Salsa, Brazilian music and Latin jazz tunes to play, since a lot of the greatest Latin music has never been put down on paper. For them, and for college-level ensembles, I have included some tunes that are not particularly "easy," and I hope that high school and middle school band directors will not find that problematic. There is plenty of material here for every level of musicianship, from novices up to professionals.

In order to make it easier to see what tunes might work for any given ensemble, we have broken the book up into "Part 1: Easier Tunes" and "Part 2: More Advanced Tunes." The songs in Part 1 should be appropriate for any high school band or even a good middle school combo, for the most part. The songs in Part 2 are a bit more challenging and are generally at the college/professional level, although more proficient high school ensembles should be able to successfully play them too. Some of them, by the way, only have one tricky part, so don't assume that all the songs in Part 2 are too difficult for your band.

THE CHARTS ARE NOT AS HARD AS THEY SEEM AT FIRST SIGHT! - Unlike earlier *Real Easy Books*, many of the songs in *The Latin Real Easy Book* have parts written out for individual players—sample bass lines, piano montunos, horn harmony parts, etc. On first glance this makes the charts seem more complicated and difficult to play. *But I believe this is a false impression.* In fact, once a player has learned his specific role in a piece of music, it makes improvising much easier than just having chord symbols to work from. Chord symbols can be realized in an infinite variety of ways, but it is often easier to make the music sound good by playing variations on a written line than it is to just improvise without any guidelines. Also, a fair number of the tunes use sixteenth-note rhythms, which might make the charts look difficult at first. But again, these rhythms aren't any harder than eighth-note rhythms once you get used to them, so hang in there!

So please do not be put off by the amount of written material in this book. Latin music is largely based on "theme and variation" and having the starting points spelled out can be a real plus, even for less-experienced players. I think band directors will find that their students will thrive on the challenge of learning their parts to these songs. This will be especially true if they are encouraged to listen to the playlists available for free at www.shermusic.com, which will bring the written music to life and make it much easier and more enjoyable to learn.

One further point of some importance: tempo markings are given on the charts to reflect the tempo of the recordings they were transcribed from. However, any of these tunes can be successfully played at significantly slower tempos, which will make them *much easier* for less experienced players to handle. Pick the tempo where it grooves! Similarly, feel free to simplify the form of the tunes if it makes it easier for your ensemble to play. For some of the songs in this book, the forms are the most complex part of the tune and can usually made simpler without ill effect.

THE CHARTS ARE OFTEN ADAPTIONS FROM THE RECORDINGS, NOT COMPLETE TRANSCRIPTIONS - Of necessity, the "Real Easy Book" format has a tune on one page (or as close as possible) and instructional material on its facing page. Because of that, especially for the Afro-Cuban tunes, we sometimes had to come up with edited versions of the tunes—i.e., sections left out, forms simplified, modulations omitted, etc. (These are indicated by saying that the chart is "adapted from the recording of....") Our transcriber, Larry Dunlap, has done a simply brilliant job of capturing the essence of these songs, but unlike *The Latin Real Book* please be forewarned that these charts may not correspond exactly with the recordings at various points.

LISTEN TO THE SONGS FOR FREE! - The intense beauty of many of the tunes is what attracts me to Latin music, and I am happy to be able to share that beauty with you via the playlists on the "Latin Real Easy Book" page of our website, www.shermusic.com. Here you will be able to hear the entire tune (not just 30 seconds) of most of the compositions in this book—an invaluable aid in being able to come up with your own interpretations of the tunes. Just a few personal favorites of mine you should check out: the unique groove on Ivan Lins' "Renata Maria," Chico Pinheino's gorgeous "There's A Storm Inside," Mario Bauza's "Así No, Papá," Descarga Boricua's version of "Que Le Den Candela," Gonzalo Teppa's haunting rendition of the Latin standard "De Repente," the late Ron Stallings' beautiful composition "Havana" (as recorded by Mark Levine's group *Que Calor*), Andy Narell's "Chakalaka," Don Grolnick's "Heart Of Darkness," Tom Jobim's "Passarim," and on and on.

In a number of cases, I have included in the playlists the version closest to the way the tune is written in this book, and then also another version or two to show you other ways the tune could be played. For the more standard tunes, however, up to a dozen versions were used as source material for these charts.

USE THE APPENDICES! - In order to help these tunes sound authentic, in Appendix 1 we have provided sample drum and percussion parts for many styles of Latin music, and some particular grooves for some of the songs. In conjunction with texts like our "The Salsa Guidebook" and "Inside The Brazilian Rhythm Section," this should be all your band's percussion section needs to sound good. Appendix II is a cogent description of how appropriate scales are chosen for common chords, which we hope you find useful. There is also a Chord Dictionary in the front of the book, in case there is any question what notes are in a given chord. Appendix III is a page of "unaltered" guitar voicings for simple seventh chords, to supplement the voicings given on p.2 of each tune. As an additional aid, our esteemed colleague Rebeca Mauleón has written an introduction to this book that will give you some ideas for taking these charts and getting the most music possible from them.

GETTING UP TO SPEED IN PLAYING LATIN MUSIC - Sher Music Co. has previously published state-of-the-art Latin fakebooks and instructional material—"The Latin Real Book," "The Brazilian Guitar Book," "The Latin Bass Book," The True Cuban Bass," "Inside The Brazilian Rhythm Section," "Introduction To The Conga Drum (DVD)," "The Conga Drummer's Guidebook," "Afro-Caribbean Grooves For Drumset," "101 Montunos," "Muy Caliente: Afro-Cuban Play-Along Book/CD," and "The Salsa Guidebook." More information on these books is available at www.shermusic.com. We suggest that students of the music study the appropriate book for their instrument in conjunction with learning the tunes in this book. *"Muy Caliente" in particular, will give any student of Latin music a great Afro-Cuban rhythm section to play-along with as they hone their soloing and/or accompanying skills.*

MANY THANKS - As with any major project, there were many people instrumental in bringing this book to fruition. So, many thanks to: Chuck Gee for another superlative music engraving job and innumerable helpful suggestions (and for the idea of this book in the first place); Larry Dunlap for his absolute brilliance and musicality in transcribing these charts from the recordings, writing most of the Supplemental Material, and for understanding what was needed to make each tune work, given our space constraints; Rebeca Mauleón for her deep knowledge of, and passion for, Latin music, which was invaluable at every stage of putting this book together; my compatriot Attila Nagy for another beautiful Sher Music cover, and Jennifer Hewitson for the great cover artwork; the publishers of the songs for their cooperation with this venture; Robert Feinberg for help with the Brazilian permissions; the crew at Ag Press in Manhattan, KS for creating the physical product you hold in your hands; my One World Band for a great time road-testing the tunes with me; Jim Nadel of the Stanford Jazz Workshop for entrusting me with the task of publishing "The Real Easy Books" in the first place; Michael Zisman for conceiving of the Real Easy Book idea; Ray Scott for his tasty guitar voicings on page 2 of each chart; Kendrick Freeman for his great work putting together the Drum/Percussion Appendix; Ricardo Peixoto for help with the Portuguese lyrics; David Schrader for the wonderful proofreading job; my gracious and understanding wife, Sueann, for everything under the sun; and finally, many thanks to the composers and performers of this amazing music for making this a better world to live in. Enjoy!

Chuck Sher, Publisher

A Note From Rebeca Mauleón

THE FEELING OF LATIN MUSIC - Anyone who loves music, studies it and plays it for a living knows there are no shortcuts to learning, only life-long commitment and lots of practice to get better. As our dear Publisher, Chuck Sher mentioned, the intention of this Latin version of the Real Easy Book series is to provide (sometimes simplified) versions of a variety of tunes that cover everything from Salsa and Brazilian music to Latin jazz. If you are new to Latin music, you probably have already discovered that there are a number of differences when it comes down to how this music is "felt" as well as played.

THE BASS - First of all, bass players need to feel comfortable with the idea in Cuban-based rhythms that the foundation is mostly syncopated, unlike the typical walking bass feel in jazz. Most of the rhythm section in Cuban music – and therefore in Salsa and Latin jazz – puts the main accents of their respective patterns on beats 2+ and 4 (what we often refer to as the *tumbao* for the bass and the *montuno* for the piano).

THE PERCUSSION SECTION - The percussion instruments are an entire world unto themselves, with many styles often containing very subtle differences within the individual rhythm patterns. So the musician really needs to have a solid command of Cuban rhythms such as *guaracha, mambo, cha-cha-chá, guajira, bolero, son, son-montuno* and so on. Within the Salsa and Latin jazz family of rhythms there are also Puerto Rican styles (*bomba* and *plena*), Dominican styles (*merengue* and *bachata*), Colombian styles (*cumbia* and *vallenato*) and so many others. Brazilian music itself contains a seemingly endless number of regional styles – from *samba* and *bossa nova* to *partido alto, forró, côco, maracatu, baião, chorinho* and more. And often what distinguishes all of these rhythms can be as subtle as what one particular drum pattern is doing. Really, every musician interpreting this music should have a reasonable understanding of these rhythms – whether they play percussion or not!

THE IMPORTANCE OF CLAVE - As most of you may also know, Cuban-based music relies on the concept of the *clave* to serve as an anchor, not only for how all the rhythm patterns are "stacked up," so to speak, but also how the arrangement is structured. In many of the tunes in this book, you will sometimes notice that the *clave* direction is specified several times within the song; this is because there are moments in an arrangement where an odd number of measures in a phrase will naturally "shift" the *clave's* direction beginning on the next musical phrase. This idea of "three-two" versus "two-three" has its roots in the West African music that is the foundation for most of the music in the Caribbean and Latin America, and it stems from the principle role of how rhythm literally shapes the melody. Until you understand what you are hearing when these *clave* changes occur, you'll be missing a big piece of the puzzle. Please see my book, *The Salsa Guidebook* (Sher Music), for more information on these topics.

THE BRAZILIAN VERSION - While Brazilian music does not necessarily contain the specific notion of the *clave*, it too is often structured around a feeling of binary patterns – a principle of tension and release that permeates much of the world's African-influenced music. The good news is that for bass players, at least, most Brazilian rhythms tend to echo a more downbeat-oriented bass line that comes from the bass drum patterns of *samba*.

GETTING THE RIGHT FEEL - All this being said, the wonderful thing is you don't necessarily need to be "advanced" as a player to grasp the basics of this music, as long as you have good, solid time and can feel comfortable in a largely syncopated environment. Perhaps the most essential ingredient of all in these genres is the improvisational nature of how the music is played. While many people think of Brazilian music, Salsa music or Latin jazz as simply a bunch of syncopated rhythm patterns, this is a language of continuous expression and improvisation.

Most of the rhythm instruments are required to maintain a fairly repetitive role as they accompany the melody, but at the same time it is important to create variations so the music doesn't feel redundant. In other words: all players in the rhythm section should follow the principle of finding the balance between stability and variation. Make it solid for the dancers, but make it fun for yourself as a player. And if you are one of the melodic instruments, your sense of phrasing in Latin music should be crisp and right on the money, not lagging behind the time. Since Latin music is largely devoid of swing feel, your interpretation of the rhythmical aspects need to tie in with the driving percussion patterns; it's got to fit like a glove and maintain that locked groove even when there are twists and turns in the arrangement. But the rhythm should also be flexible, not mechanical. A great way to think about "feel" in

Latin music is to practice an exercise of playing three against two in 6/8 meter (as well as two against three), as written here:

This way of phrasing is common because of the prominence of compound meter and cross rhythms in West Africa, so the more comfort level you have with these rhythmical ideas, the more solid your Latin music chops will become.

Finally, there is no element more important than your own ears to get you to <u>feel</u> Latin rhythms. LISTEN to as much of this music as you can; take some dance lessons, learn to play a *conga* drum, a *surdo* or a cowbell. The more you immerse yourself in this world the more you will know that good rhythm is the key.

SOME NOTES TO BAND DIRECTORS - Sample bass, piano and other instrument patterns are generally given on the right-hand page facing each tune as a guideline. As mentioned earlier, it is implicit in the approach to playing Latin music that the player should evolve the patterns over time by creating variations, but beginning level players may wish to concentrate on the provided patterns first. Before running the tune, I recommend starting with the main repeated section of the song (if there is one). Try having the players lock into a groove and experiment with variations, and then allow the melodic players to take turns soloing over the chord changes. Since this portion of the song tends to be the most vibrant in terms of dynamics, it is a good strategy to let the musicians find the comfort zone of the groove before working on the overall structure of the song.

If you are working with vocalists, it is the repeated refrain of songs in the Cuban or Salsa genres that would also require tweaking, in that the lead vocalist needs to improvise in between the repeated chorus. This refrain section is also referred to as the *montuno*, and it is here where the ensemble will need to work on changing the *comping* (accompaniment) patterns to suit the mood. There are different approaches for the rhythm section depending on whether there are call-and-response vocals versus an instrumental solo, and often these changes are dictated by the *timbales* player (and/or drummer).

RHYTHM SECTION SUGGESTIONS - The general rule for rhythm section dynamics within a song is similar to most popular music in that the drummer(s) create subtle to wide-ranging dynamic changes between sections: softer during the verses, louder during the solos and everywhere in between. But in Cuban-based music, the *timbales* tend to drive the band with specific calls, fills and breaks, and there are generally three areas of the set that coincide with various sections of the songs: a) during the verses, the *timbales* player plays the *cáscara* (sides of the drums), sometimes with the *clave* pattern on a woodblock; b) during the call-and-response vocals, the *timbales* player and *bongo* player play an interlocking cowbell part (these patterns can be shared and also morphed into a 2-bell part played by one drummer), and c) during higher dynamic instrumental solos (trumpet, sax, electric guitar, etc...) the drummer will play the ride cymbal.

For piano and bass solos, however, the drummer typically plays the sides of the drums (*cáscara*), and for percussion solos the cowbell pattern is a must to anchor the time. There are certainly exceptions and variations to all of these "rules," so it is highly recommended that all of the players listen to the recordings found on the playlists of the Latin Real Easy Book page of www.shermusic.com to hear how the rhythm section responds during each section. Drum-set players tend to try to adopt all of the traditional percussion patterns onto the set, and that can be daunting as well as slightly inappropriate, mainly because there are several ways to interpret the specific Latin music styles that are more creative and not necessarily literal. Again, depending on your particular rhythm section, the suggested approach is to be sure to lock in all of the rhythm parts before launching into playing the tune. Once the groove is solid, it will be much easier to put all of the pieces of the puzzle together. Finding the tight rhythmical "zone" is the cornerstone to all Latin music interpretation. If it feels right, the audience will want to dance!

A Note from the Music Editor

THIS NEWEST ENTRY IN THE REAL EASY SERIES, at first glance, might seem a bit daunting and difficult. In general, Latin music tends to be more complex than the "real easy" jazz tunes in the earlier volumes of this series. Don't be scared away. Latin music is very rewarding and a great addition to a jazz musician's repertoire.

Salsa Music, whether of Cuban, Puerto Rican or other origin, tends to embrace forms that are longer and more complex than a 16 or 32 measure standard or a 12 bar blues. The tunes often have several sections as well as solo sections (most often vamps) that are separate from the main melody sections.

Brazilian music tends to have more advanced harmonic structures and harmonies and often longer song forms than the simple jazz compositions.

All Latin styles have distinct and specific rhythmic feels. Though they may be unfamiliar and a little difficult at first, with some practice these rhythms will become as natural as swing and other more common jazz feels.

AN EXCELLENT BASIS FOR MASTERING THESE STYLES can be found in the Latin music instructional books mentioned in Chuck Sher's Introduction. Rebeca Mauleón's Introduction in the previous pages is a good start. And don't ignore the fantastic playlists Chuck has put on The Latin Real Easy Book page at www.shermusic.com. Listening is the best education.

THE SAMPLE PIANO VOICINGS AND BASS LINES in the Supplemental Material for each chart were generally based on what I heard on the recordings of the specific tunes. The main exception to this is that Rebeca wrote out piano montunos that will be more playable by developing players.

AN INTRODUCTION TO SCALES in Appendix II is a very basic approach to learning what scales you might wish to consider when improvising. This short article will explain why some notes are printed in black and some in white in the scales you find in the Supplemental Material on the second pages of charts.

HAVE FUN WITH THESE TUNES! There are many wonderful compositions included in this book. Groove to the music and remember this is primarily music for dancing and moving. Find your own way to make this music live in you.

THANKS! As always, big thanks to Chuck Sher, Chuck Gee, Rebeca Mauleón and everyone else who made this book possible. Special thanks to my lovely wife, Bobbe Norris, for putting up with my somewhat eccentric work "routine." It has been an inspiring joy working on getting this music out.

Larry Dunlap, Music Editor

Chord Dictionary

The chord symbols in this book follow (with some exceptions) the system outlined in *Standard Chord Symbol Notation* by Carl Brandt and Clinton Roemer. It is hoped you will find them clear, complete and unambiguous.

Below are two groups of chord spelling:

a) The full range of chords normally encountered, given a C root. Transpose them to whatever root you need.

b) The bottom three lines show some more unusual chords—slash chords, chords with omitted notes, etc.

xi

REBECA MAULEÓN

PART 1:
EASIER TUNES

Agua De Beber

Music by Antonio Carlos Jobim
Lyric by Vinicius de Moraes
English lyric by Norman Gimbel

Solo on Tune (A B)
(play letter C as is each x)
After solos, D.S. al Coda

2

SUPPLEMENTAL MATERIAL - Agua De Beber

Scales for Soloing (for chords with alterations)

Sample Piano Voicings

Sample Bass

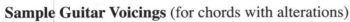

Sample Guitar Voicings (for chords with alterations)

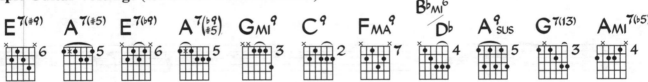

Extra Lyrics

(Letter A, 3rd verse)
Eu sempre tive uma certeza
Que só me deu desilusão
E que o amor é uma tristeza
Multa mágoa demais para um coração

English Lyric (Letter A, 1st verse)
Your love is rain, my heart the flower
I need your love or I will die.
My very life is in your power
Will I wither and fade or bloom to the sky?

(Letter A - 2nd verse)
The rain can fall on distant deserts.
The rain can fall upon the sea.
The rain can fall upon the flower.
Since the rain has to fall, let it fall on me.

(Chorus)
Agua de beber,
Give the flower water to drink.
Agua de beber
Give the flower water to drink.

Around The Corner

Bright Samba (♩ = 106)

Larry Dunlap

Based on the chord changes of "Samba de Orpheu."

SUPPLEMENTAL MATERIAL - Around The Corner

Scales for Soloing

Sample Piano Voicings

Sample Comping Rhythm

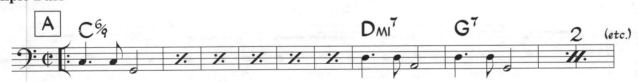

Sample Bass

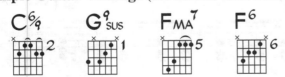

Sample Guitar Voicings (for chords with alterations)

Berimbau

Music by Baden Powell
Lyric by Vinicius de Moraes

Quem é ho-nem de bem não trai___ o a-mor que lhe quer seu bem.___

___ Quem diz mui-to que vai, não vai,___ é as-sim co-mo não vai, não vem.___

___ Quem de den-tro de si não sai___ vai mor-rer sem a-mar nin-guém.___

___ O di-nhei-ro de quem não dá___ é o tra-ba-lho de quem não tem.___

___ Ca-po-ei-ra que é bom não cai,___ mas se um di-a e-le cai, cai bem.

Ca- po- ei- ra me___ man-dou___ di- zer que já che-gou,___ che-

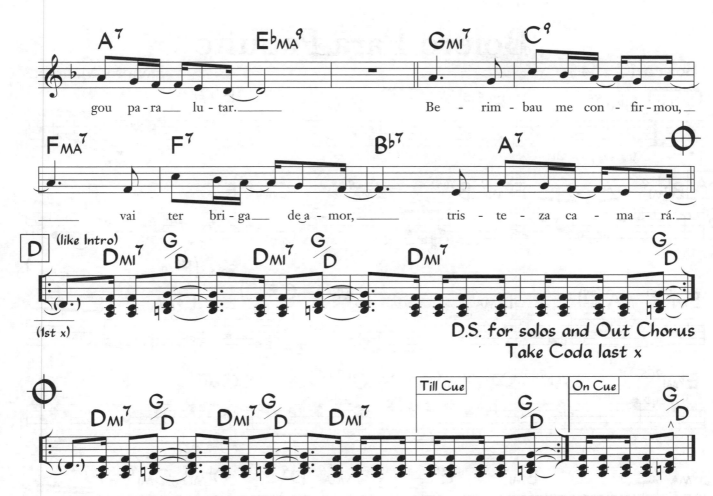

goa pa-ra lu-tar. Be - rim-bau me con - fir-mou,
vai ter bri-ga de_a-mor, tris-te-za ca-ma-rá.

D (like Intro)

D.S. for solos and Out Chorus
Take Coda last x

(1st x)

Till Cue On Cue

The chords in parentheses in letter A are the original chords, but the "primary" chords are often used.

SUPPLEMENTAL MATERIAL - Berimbau

Selected Scales for Soloing

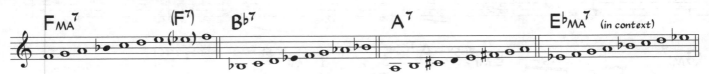

Sample Piano Voicings

Sample Bass

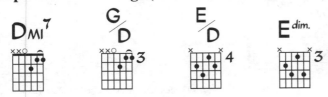

Sample Guitar Voicings (for chords with alterations)

Bolero Para Paquito

Hendrik Meurkens

Solo on Tune (A B)
After solos, D.S. al Coda

SUPPLEMENTAL MATERIAL - Bolero Para Paquito

Scales for Soloing (for chords with alterations)

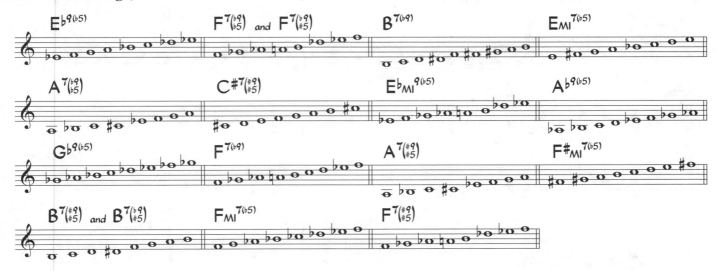

Sample Piano Voicings (for chords with alterations)

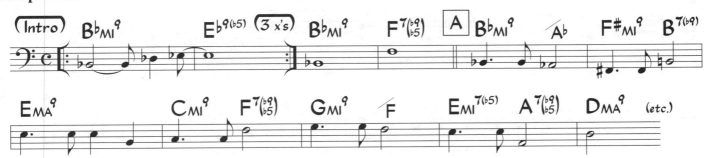

Sample Bass

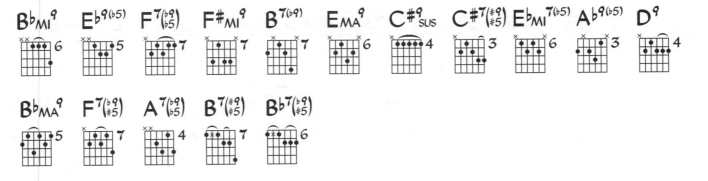

Sample Guitar Voicings (for chords with alterations)

Caballo Viejo

Charanga - Vallenata (♩ = 94-118)
"2-3 Clave Feel"

Simon Diaz
(adapted from Roberto Torres' recording)

A

Cuan - do el a - mor ___ lle - ga a - sí ___ de es - ta ma - ne - ra, u -

no no se ___ da ni cuen - ta. ___ El

ca'u - tal re - ver - de - ce y el ___ gua - na - chi - to ___ flo - re - ce y la

so - ga se ___ re - vien - ta. ___ - ta. ___ Ca -

B

ba - llo le dan sa - ba - na por - que es - tá vie - jo y can - sao', ___ pe -
si u - na po - tra a - la - za - na ca - ba - llo vie - jo se en - cuen - tra el

ro no se dan de cuen - ta que un ___ co - ra - zón a - ma - rrao' cuan -
pe - cho se le des - gra - na y ___ no le ha - ce ca - so a fal - se - ta y

do le suel - tan la rein - da es ___ ca - ba - llo des - bo - cao'.
no l'o - be - de - ce a fre - no ni ___ lo pa - ra un pa - sa - rien -

Y ___ da.

D.S. al Coda
(w/ repeats)

©1983 Barnegat Music, as agent of Selemusica S.A.
Used by Permission.

10

Cuan - do el a - mor lle - ga a - sí, lle - ga a - sí, de es - ta ma - ne - ra.

Ca - ba - llo le dan sa - ba -

- na por que es - tá vie - jo y___ can - sao',___

Ca -

D.S.S. (to letter C) al Fine

SUPPLEMENTAL MATERIAL - Caballo Viejo

Scales for Soloing

Note: These two scales are the same. Stress the chord tones to distinguish the two scales.

Extra Lyrics for D.S.

(Letter A both times on D.S.)
Cuando el amor llega así de esta manera uno no tiene la culpa.
Quererse no tiene horarios ni fecha en el calendario quando las ganas se juntan.

(1st **x**, Letter B on D.S.)
Caballo le dan sabana
y tiene el tiempo contao'
y se va por la mañana
con su pasito apurao'
a verse con su potranca
que lo tiene embatbascao'

(2nd **x**, Letter B on D.S.)
El potro da tiempo al tiempo
porque le sobra la edad.
Caballo viejo no puede
perder la flor que le dan
porque después de esta vida
no hay otra oportunidad.

Caballo Viejo (rhythm section)

12

SUPPLEMENTAL MATERIAL - Caballo Viejo

Scales for Soloing

Note: These two scales are the same. Stress the chord tones to distinguish the two scales.

Sample Guitar Voicings (for chord with alterations)

$E_{MI}^{7(b5)}$

Cafe Rio

Bossa Nova (♩ = 112)

Larry Dunlap

Based on the chord changes of "The Girl From Ipanema."

14

SUPPLEMENTAL MATERIAL - Cafe Rio

Scales for Soloing

Sample Piano Voicings

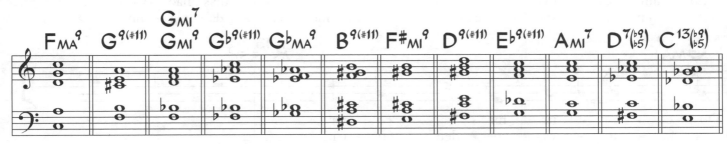

Sample Bass

Sample Guitar Voicings (for chords with alterations)

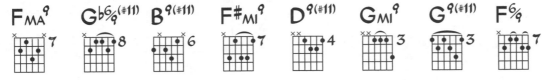

Camaleão

SUPPLEMENTAL MATERIAL - Camaleão

Scales for Soloing (for chords with alterations)

Sample Piano Voicings

Sample Bass

Sample Percussion (for Intro and letter A, 1st x)

Sample Guitar Comp Rhythm

Sample Guitar Voicings (for chords with alterations)

Cha-cha-chá (♩ = 152)

Chucho

Paquito d'Rivera

Go on to letter B for solos

Repeat letter B for more solos.
After solos, D.S. al Fine (w/ repeat).

SUPPLEMENTAL MATERIAL - Chucho

Scales for Soloing

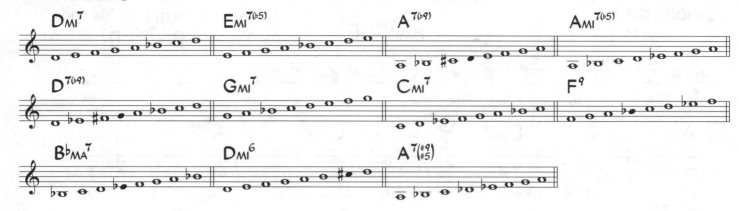

Sample Piano Voicings

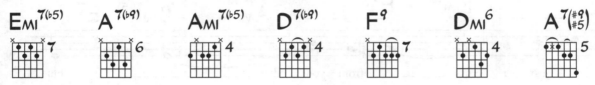

Sample Guitar Voicings (for chords with alterations)

Emi⁷⁽ᵇ⁵⁾ 7   A⁷⁽ᵇ⁹⁾ 6   Ami⁷⁽ᵇ⁵⁾ 4   D⁷⁽ᵇ⁹⁾ 4   F⁹ 7   Dmi⁶ 4   A⁷⁽#⁹#⁵⁾ 5

SUPPLEMENTAL MATERIAL - A Day In The Life Of A Fool

Scales for Soloing (for chords with alterations)

Sample Piano Voicings

Sample Bass

Sample Guitar Voicings (for chords with alterations)

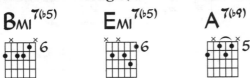

De Repente

South American $\frac{6}{8}$ Feel (Joropo)
Slow & Sultry or Bright
(various tempos)

Aldemaro Romero

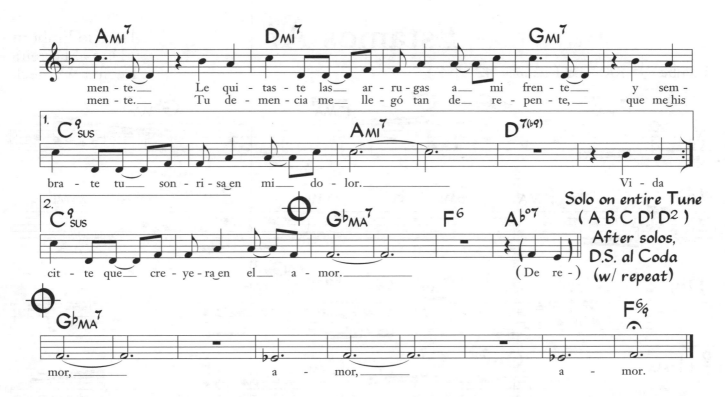

men - te.___ Le qui - tas - te las ar - ru - gas a mi fren - te y sem -
men - te.___ Tu de - men - cia me lle - gó tan de re - pen - te,___ que me his

bra - te tu___ son - ri - sa en mi do - lor.___

Vi - da

cit - te que___ cre - ye - ra en el a - mor.___

Solo on entire Tune
(A B C D¹ D²)
After solos,
D.S. al Coda
(w/ repeat)
(De re -)

mor,___ a - mor, a - mor.

SUPPLEMENTAL MATERIAL - De Repente

Scales for Soloing (for chords with alterations)

Sample Piano Voicings

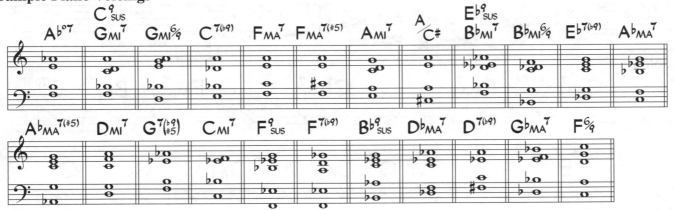

Sample Bass

Sample Guitar Voicings (for chords with alterations)

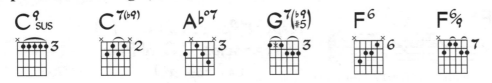

Estamos Aí

SUPPLEMENTAL MATERIAL - Estamos Aí

Scales for Soloing (for chords with alterations)

Sample Piano Voicings

Sample Bass (for solos)

Repeat for Solos
(D E F¹ F²)

Sample Guitar Voicings (for chords with alterations)

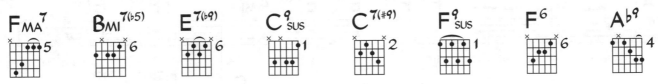

Inolvidable

Julio Gutierrez
(adapted from Tito Rodriguez' recording)

SUPPLEMENTAL MATERIAL - Inolvidable

Scales for Soloing (for chords with alterations)

Sample Piano Voicings (for chords with alterations)

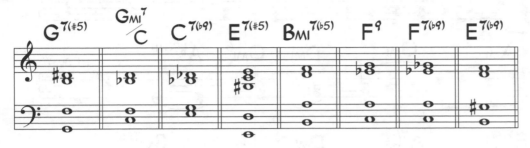

Sample Bolero Piano Comping

Sample Bass

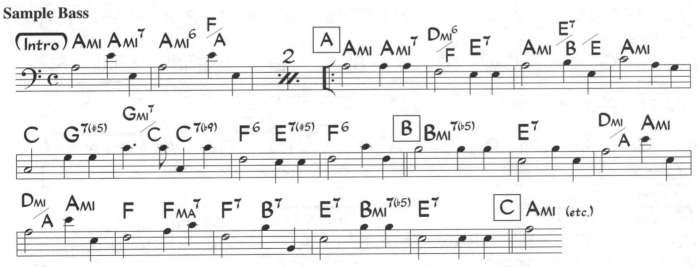

Sample Guitar Voicings (for chords with alterations)

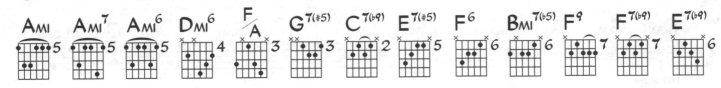

SUPPLEMENTAL MATERIAL - La Cuna

Scales for Soloing (in D minor context)

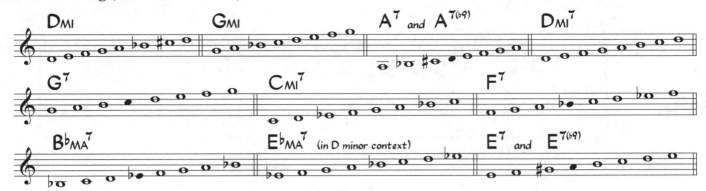

Sample Piano Montunos   (at Letters A, C, and Coda, 1st section)

(both hands)

(at Letter E, and Coda, 2nd section)

(both hands)

Sample Piano Voicings (for chords with alterations)

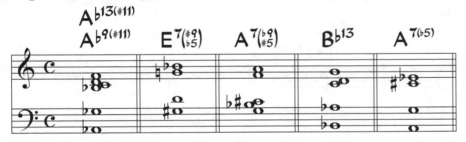

Sample Bass

Sample Guitar Voicings (for chords with alterations)

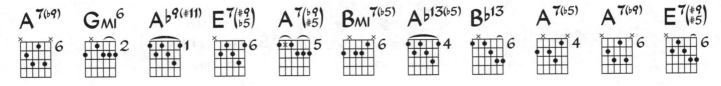

(Se Acabó) La Malanga

Rudy Calzado
(adapted from Eddie Palmieri's recording)

SUPPLEMENTAL MATERIAL - (Se Acabó) La Malanga

Scales for Soloing

Sample Piano Voicings

Sample Piano Montunos

Sample Bass Tumbaos

Sample Guitar Voicings (for chords with alterations)

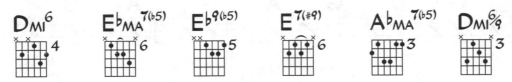

Ca - mi - na   co - mo Chen - cha la___ Gam - bá.

(Vamp & solo till cue)

(fl.)

tutti_____

SUPPLEMENTAL MATERIAL - La Mujer De Antonio

Scales for Soloing (in context of D major)

Sample Bass

(etc.)

Sample Guitar Voicings (for chords with alterations)

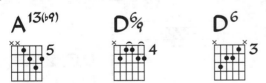

La Mujer De Antonio (rhythm section)

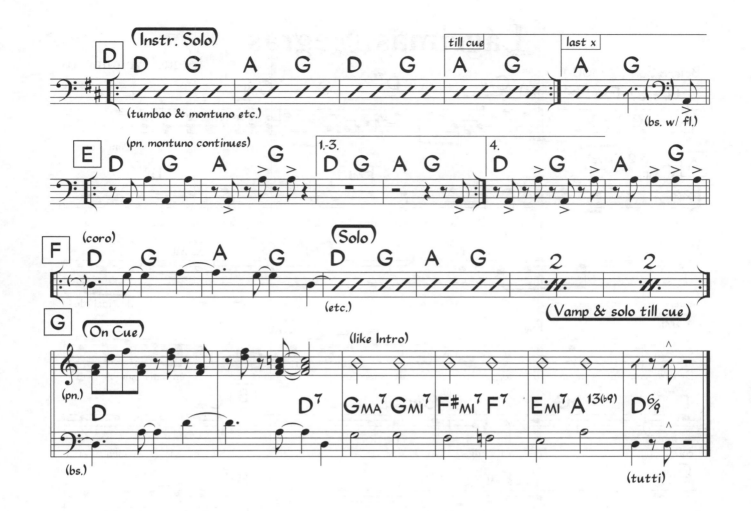

SUPPLEMENTAL MATERIAL - La Mujer De Antonio

Scales for Soloing (in context of D major)

Sample Bass Tumbao (measure 5 of Letter B through Letter D)

Sample Guitar Voicings (for chords with alterations)

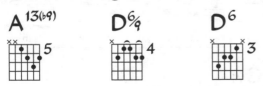

Lágrimas Negras

Miguel Matamoros

SUPPLEMENTAL MATERIAL - Lágrimas Negras

Scales for Soloing

Sample Piano Voicings

Sample Piano Montuno

Sample Bass

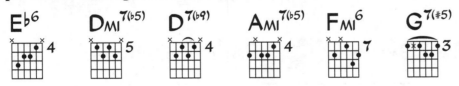

Sample Guitar Voicings (for chords with alterations)

SUPPLEMENTAL MATERIAL - Lamento

Scales for Soloing (for chords with alterations)

Sample Piano Voicings

Sample Bass

Sample Guitar Voicings (for chords with alterations)

Let's Go Dancing

Victor Feldman

40

Melody is originally played by flute one octave higher than written. Use chords in parentheses for solos.
Bass plays Samba 2 through letter B for solos. Break in bar 16 of letter A is omitted for solos.

SUPPLEMENTAL MATERIAL - Let's Go Dancing

Scales for Soloing (for chords with alterations)

Sample Piano Voicings

Sample Bass

Sample Guitar Voicings (for chords with alterations)

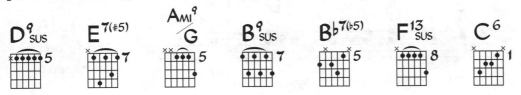

Liberated Brother

Weldon Irvine
(as recorded by Horace Silver)

42

SUPPLEMENTAL MATERIAL - Liberated Brother

Scales for Soloing (for chords with alterations)

Sample Piano Voicings

Sample Piano for Head

(plus 8va b.)

(plus 8va b.)

Sample Bass

Sample Guitar Voicings (for chords with alterations)

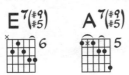

Little Sunflower

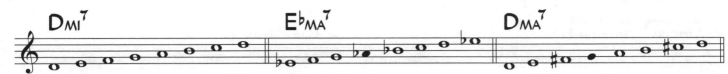

SUPPLEMENTAL MATERIAL - Little Sunflower

Scales for Soloing

Sample Piano Voicings

Sample Bass

Solo on Tune (A¹ A² B¹ B²)
After solos, D.S. al Coda
(w/ repeats)

(alternate pattern)

Sample Guitar Voicings

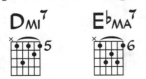

Little Sunflower (harmony parts for melody)

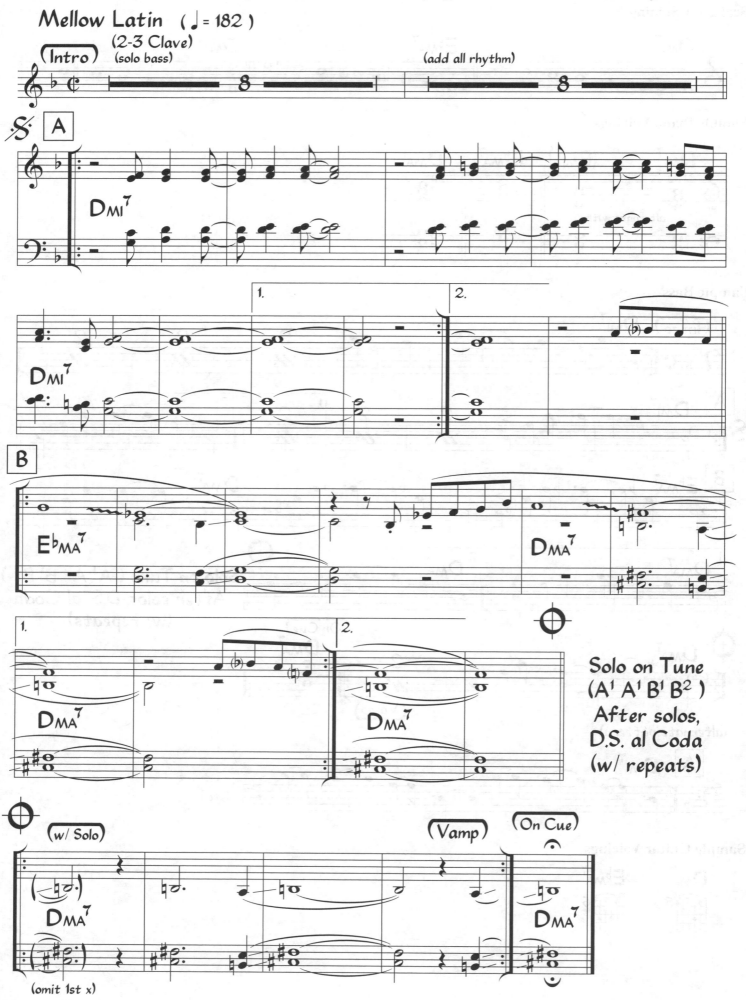

(background horn parts for solos)

SUPPLEMENTAL MATERIAL - Little Sunflower

Scales for Soloing

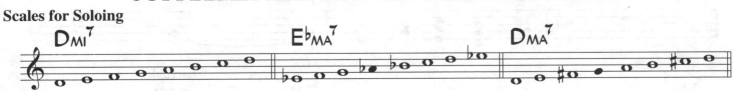

The Long Way Back

Bright Baião (♩ = 130 - 132)

Andy Narell
(adapted from the original recording)

D.S. for solos
Solo on Tune (A B C)
After solos, D.S. al Coda

(Vamp till cue)

SUPPLEMENTAL MATERIAL - The Long Way Back

Scales for Soloing (for chords with alterations)

Sample Piano Voicings

Sample Bass

Sample Guitar Voicings (for chords with alterations)

Lugar Comum

João Donato
Gilberto Gil

This chart is based on João Donato's recorded version. However, he performs this in Db.
It is written here in C for easier playing.

SUPPLEMENTAL MATERIAL - Lugar Comum

Scales for Soloing

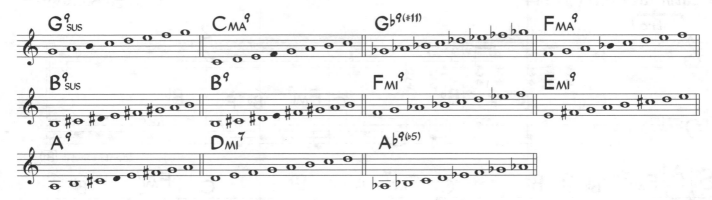

Sample Piano Voicings

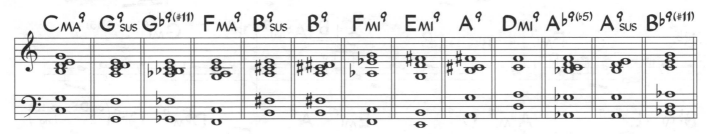

Sample Bass

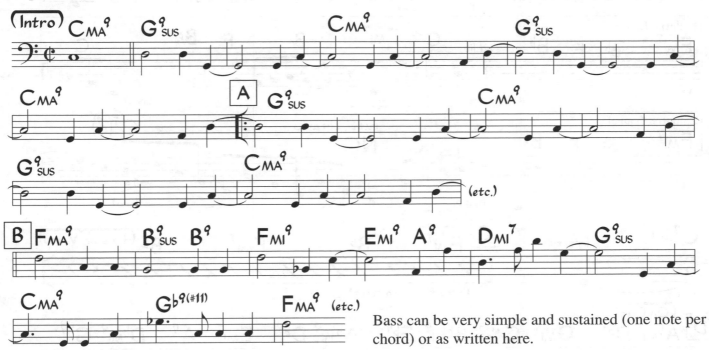

Bass can be very simple and sustained (one note per chord) or as written here.

Sample Guitar Voicings (for chords with alterations)

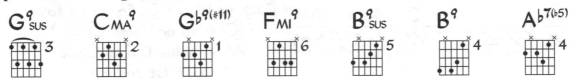

My Latin Brother

SUPPLEMENTAL MATERIAL - My Latin Brother

Scales for Soloing

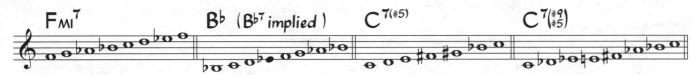

Sample Piano Voicings

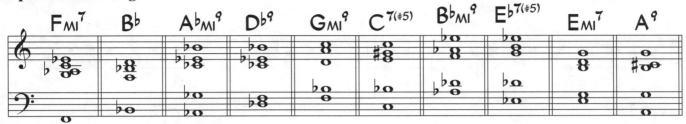

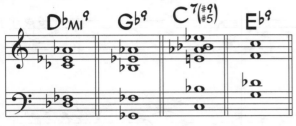

Sample Bass

Sample Guitar Voicings (for chords with alterations)

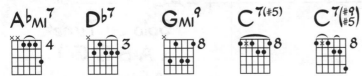

Nana

Medium Cha-cha-chá (♩ = 162)

Moacir Santos
(as recorded by Mark Levine and The Latin Tinge)

Solo on Tune
(A B C C)
After solos,
D.C. al Coda
(no repeat)

Disregard rhythm anticipations and figures during solos.

SUPPLEMENTAL MATERIAL - Nana

Scales for Soloing

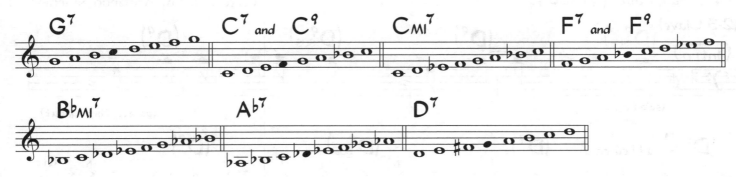

Sample Piano Voicings

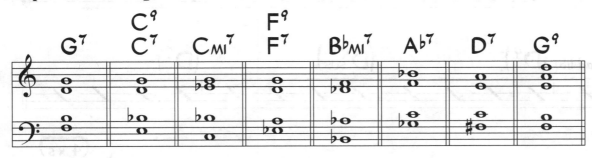

Sample Bass (for head)

Sample Guitar Voicings (for chords with alterations)

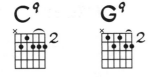

Pa' Gozar

SUPPLEMENTAL MATERIAL - Pa' Gozar

Scales for Soloing

The only difference in these scales is the alternation of F♯ and G.

Sample Piano Voicings (used only for comping during bass solo)

(Left-hand voicings for piano solo)

Sample Guitar Voicings (for chords with alterations)

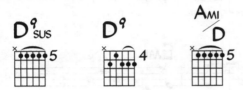

Pare Cochero

Miguel Angel Banguela
Marcelino Guerra
(adapted from Orquesta Aragon's recording)

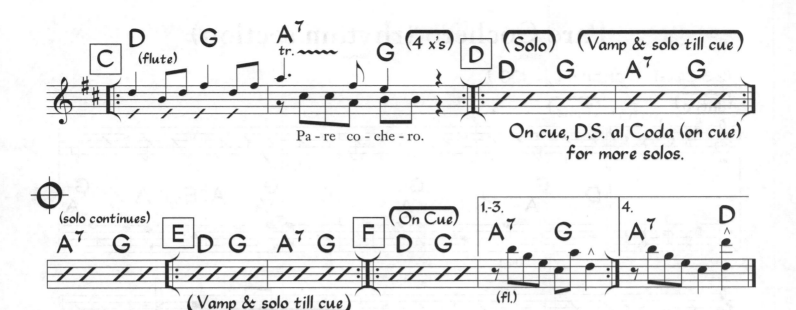

SUPPLEMENTAL MATERIAL - Pare Cochero

Scales for Soloing

Note: All these scales have the same notes. Only the "avoid" notes distinguish them. The entire solo section(s) can be approached as a "D major scale," being aware of the "avoid" notes of the different scales.

Sample Piano Voicings

Sample Piano Montuno

Sample Guitar Voicings (for chords with alterations)

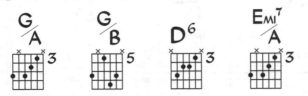

59

Pare Cochero (rhythm section)

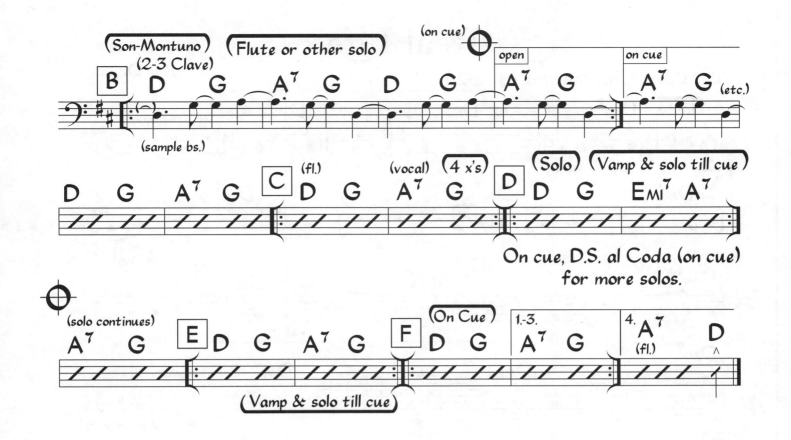

On cue, D.S. al Coda (on cue)
for more solos.

SUPPLEMENTAL MATERIAL - Pare Cochero

Scales for Soloing

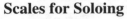

Note: All these scales have the same notes. Only the "avoid" notes distinguish them. The entire solo section(s) can be approached as a "D major scale," being aware of the "avoid" notes of the different scales.

Sample Piano Voicings

Sample Piano Montuno

Sample Guitar Voicings

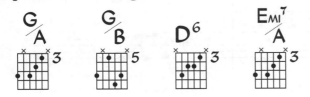

Real Life

Ray Obiedo

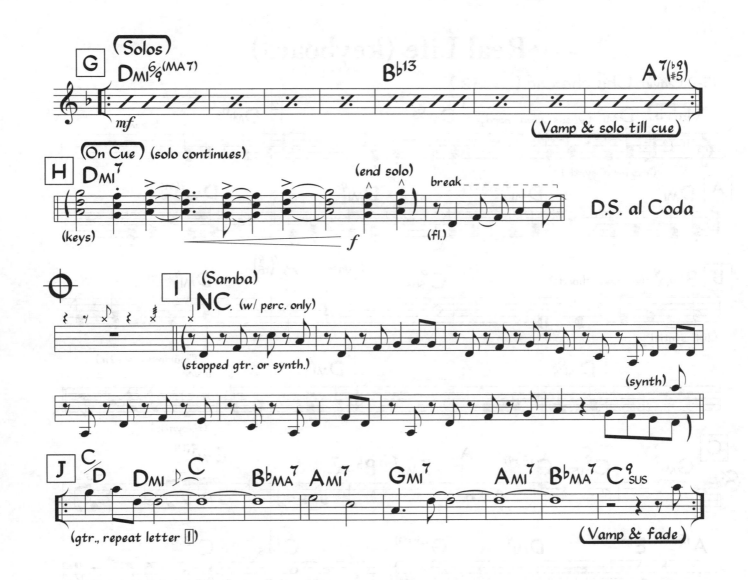

SUPPLEMENTAL MATERIAL - Real Life

Scales for Soloing

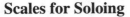

Sample Guitar Voicings (for chords with alterations)

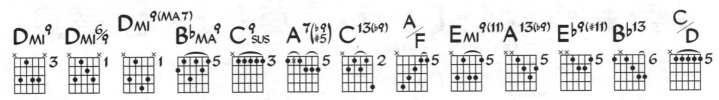

Real Life (keyboard)

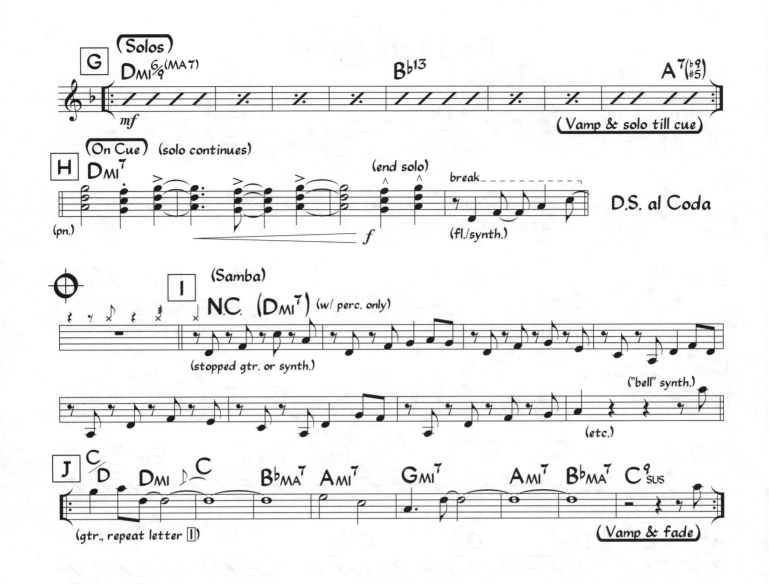

SUPPLEMENTAL MATERIAL - Real Life

Scales for Soloing

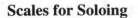

Sample Piano Voicings

Real Life (bass)

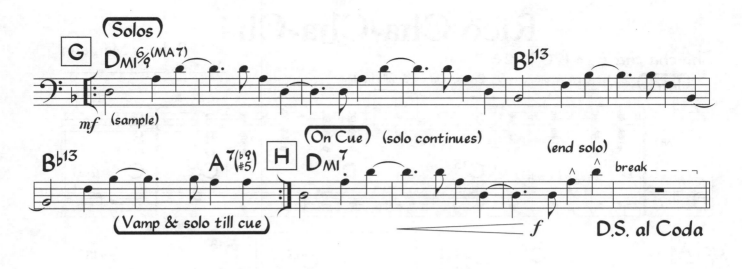

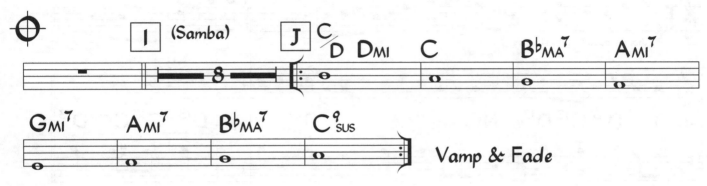

Vamp & Fade

SUPPLEMENTAL MATERIAL - Real Life

Scales for Soloing

Sample Guitar Voicings (for chords with alterations)

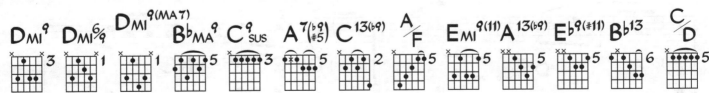

Rico Cha-Cha-Chá

Rebeca Mauleón

Based on the chord changes to "Oye Como Va."

Scales for Soloing

Sample Piano Montuno

Sample Guitar Voicings

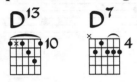

Rico Vacilón

Rosendo Ruiz

SUPPLEMENTAL MATERIAL - Rico Vacilón

Scales for Soloing

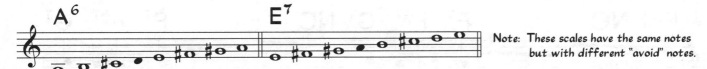

Note: These scales have the same notes but with different "avoid" notes.

Sample Piano Montuno (at Letters A and C to the end)

(both hands)

(etc.)

Sample Bass

(etc.)

Sample Guitar Voicings (for chords with alterations)

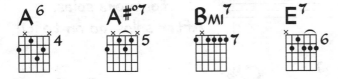

Extra Lyrics

2nd Verse (Letter B, 2nd x)
Unas sueñan con capa de armiño,
otras quieren un televisión,
hay algunas que piden castillo,
pero todas gozan el vacilón.

3rd Verse (Letter B, 3rd x)
Unas tienan la cara bonita,
otras tienen naríz de ratón,
las hay gordas, también delgaditas,
pero todas gozan el vacilón.

Ritmo Remo

David Torres
Ildefonso Sanchez
(adapted from Poncho Sanchez' recording)

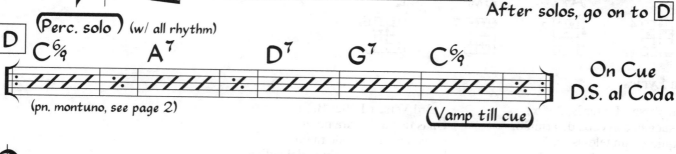

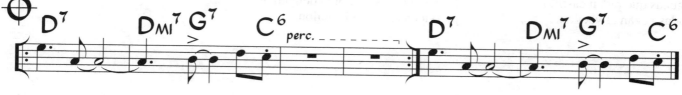

Based on the chord changes of "Take The 'A' Train"

SUPPLEMENTAL MATERIAL - Ritmo Remo

Scales for Soloing (for chords with alterations)

Sample Piano Voicings

Sample Piano Montuno (during percussion solo at Letter D)

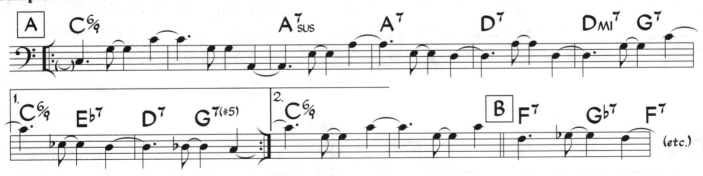

Sample Bass

Sample Guitar Voicings (for chords with alterations)

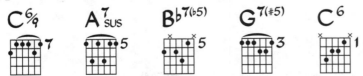

Rua Bougainville

SUPPLEMENTAL MATERIAL - Rua Bougainville

Scales for Soloing (for chords with alterations)

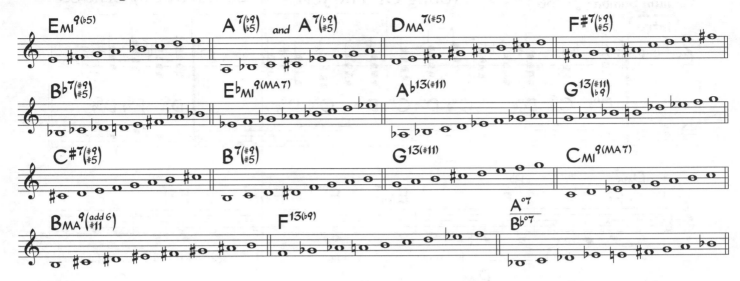

Sample Piano Voicings (for chords with alterations)

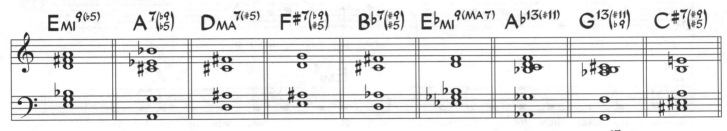

Sample Bass

Sample Guitar Voicings (for chords with alterations)

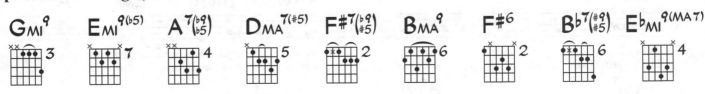

Samba Do Avião
(Song Of The Jet)

Antonio Carlos Jobim
English lyric by Gene Lees

* This is also performed faster or slower.

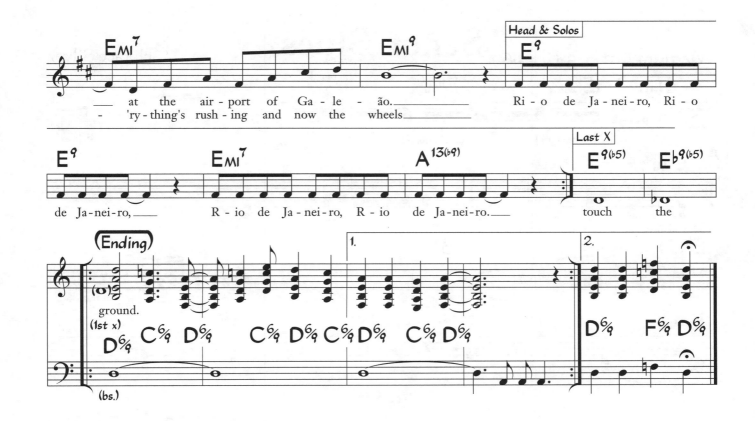

at the air-port of Ga-le-ão.＿＿＿ Ri-o de Ja-nei-ro, Ri-o
-'ry-thing's rush-ing and now the wheels＿＿＿

de Ja-nei-ro,＿＿ R-io de Ja-nei-ro, R-io de Ja-nei-ro.＿＿ touch the

ground.
(1st x)

SUPPLEMENTAL MATERIAL - Samba Do Avião

Scales for Soloing (for chords with alterations)

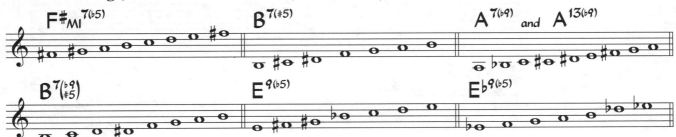

Sample Piano Voicings

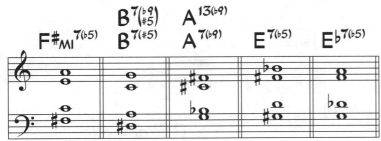

Sample Bass

Sample Guitar Voicings (for chords with alterations)

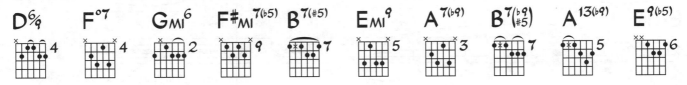

Señor Blues

Horace Silver

SUPPLEMENTAL MATERIAL - Señor Blues

Scales for Soloing

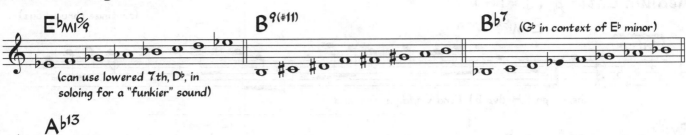

(can use lowered 7th, D♭, in soloing for a "funkier" sound)

(G♭ in context of E♭ minor)

Sample Piano Voicings

Sample Guitar Voicings (for chords with alterations)

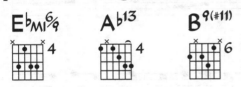

Señor Blues (rhythm section)

Bass and piano continue figure throughout head and solos.

SUPPLEMENTAL MATERIAL - Señor Blues

Scales for Soloing

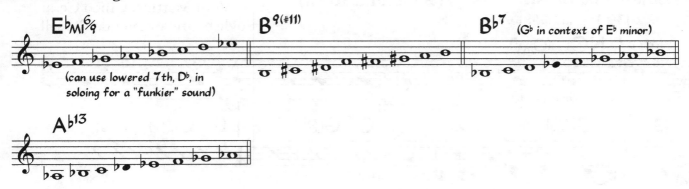

(can use lowered 7th, Db, in soloing for a "funkier" sound)

Sample Piano Voicings

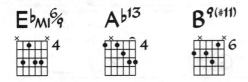

Sample Guitar Voicings (for chords with alterations)

She Walks This Earth
(Soberana Rosa)

Music by Ivan Lins
Portuguese lyric by
Vitor Martins, Chico Cesar
English lyric by Brenda Russell

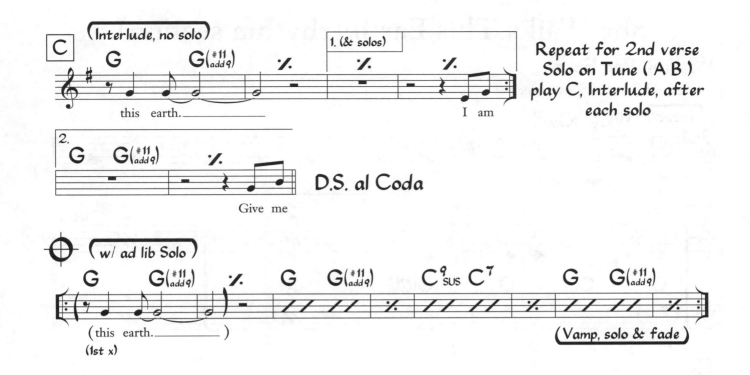

SUPPLEMENTAL MATERIAL - She Walks This Earth

Scales for Soloing

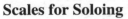

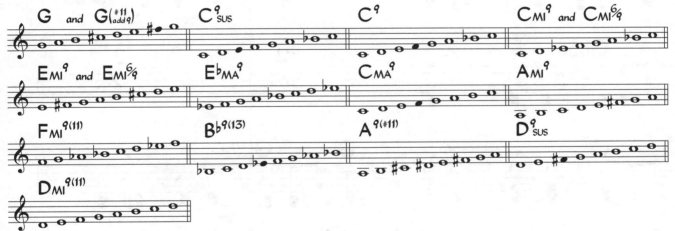

Sample Piano Voicings

Sample Guitar Voicings (for chords with alterations)

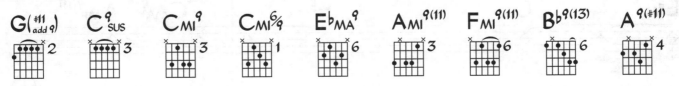

She Walks This Earth (rhythm section)

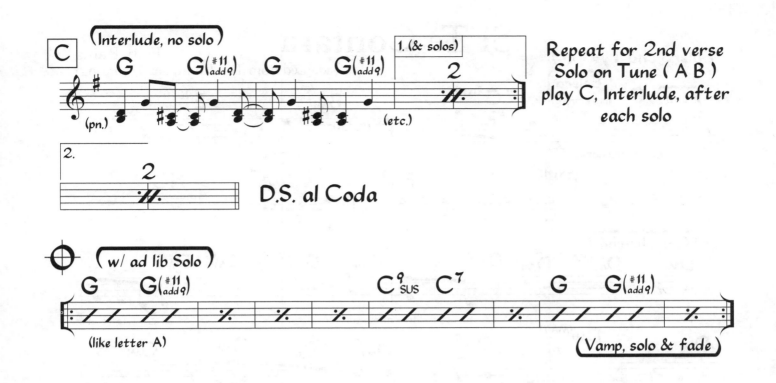

Repeat for 2nd verse
Solo on Tune (A B)
play C, Interlude, after
each solo

D.S. al Coda

SUPPLEMENTAL MATERIAL - She Walks This Earth

Scales for Soloing (in the context of this song)

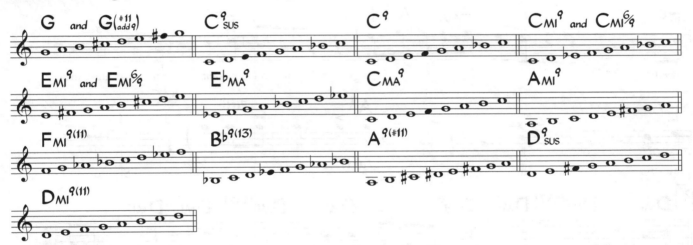

Sample Piano Voicings

Sample Guitar Voicings (for chords with alterations)

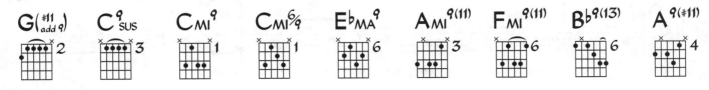

85

Si Te Contara

Felix Reina
(adapted from Tito Rodriguez' recording)

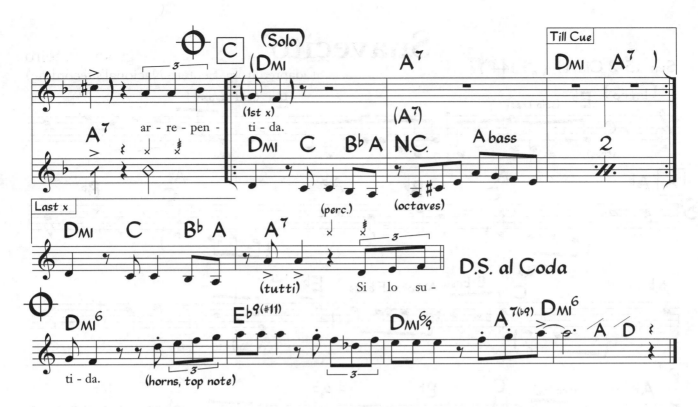

SUPPLEMENTAL MATERIAL - Si Te Contara

Sample Piano Voicings (except triads at letter C)

Sample Bass

Sample Piano Comping

Scales for Soloing (at letter C)

Selected Sample Guitar Voicings (for chords with alterations)

Suavecito

Ignacio Piñeiro
(adapted from Septeto Nacional's recording)

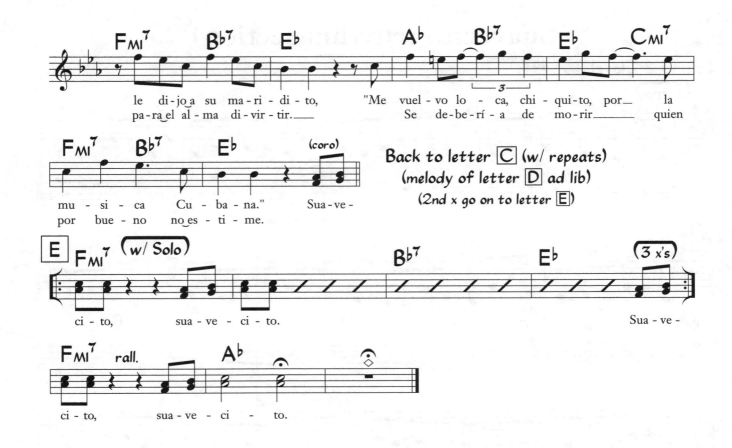

le di-jo a su ma-ri-di-to, "Me vuel-vo lo-ca, chi-qui-to, por___ la
pa-ra el al-ma di-vir-tir.___ Se de-be-rí-a de mo-rir_____ quien

Back to letter C (w/ repeats)
(melody of letter D ad lib)
(2nd x go on to letter E)

mu-si-ca Cu-ba-na." Sua-ve-
por bue-no no es-ti-me.

ci-to, sua-ve-ci-to. Sua-ve-

ci-to, sua-ve-ci-to.

SUPPLEMENTAL MATERIAL - Suavecito

Scales for Soloing

Note: The 3 scales are identical, but with different "avoid" notes.

Sample Piano Voicings

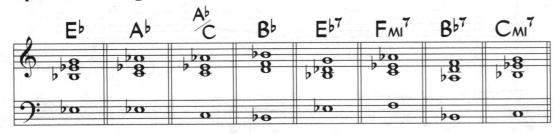

Sample Guitar Voicings (for chords with alterations)

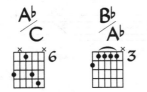

Suavecito (rhythm section)

Back to letter C (w/ repeats)
(melody of letter D ad lib)
(2nd x go on to letter E)

SUPPLEMENTAL MATERIAL - Suavecito

Scales for Soloing

Note: The 3 scales are identical, but with different "avoid" notes.

Sample Piano Voicings

Sample Guitar Voicings (for chords with alterations)

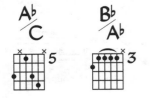

This Happy Madness
(Estrada Branca)

Antonio Carlos Jobim
English lyric by Gene Lees

Ballad (ala Classical)
(see page 2)

call this hap-py mad-ness that I feel in-side of me, some kind of wild Oc-to-ber glad-ness that I

ne-ver thought I'd see? What has be-come of all my sad-ness, all my end-less lone-ly sighs? Where are my

sor-rows now? What hap-pened to the frown, and is that self-con-tent-ed

clown stand-ing there grin-ning in the mir-ror real-ly me? I'd like to run thru Cen-tral

Park, carve your in-i-tials in the bark of ev-'ry tree I pass for ev-'ry-one to

see. I feel that I've gone back to child-hood and I'm skip-ping thru the wild-wood; so ex-

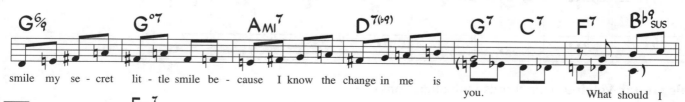

cit-ed that I don't know what to do. What do I care if I'm a ju-ven-ile? I

smile my se-cret lit-tle smile be-cause I know the change in me is you. What should I

call this hap-py mad-ness, all this un-ex-pect-ed joy that turned the world in-to a ba-by's bounc-ing

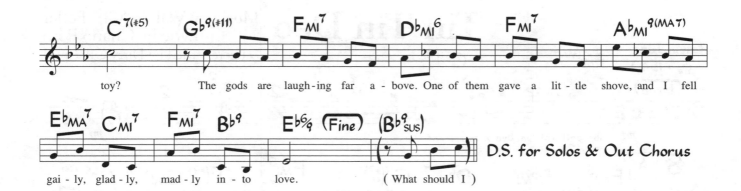

toy? The gods are laugh-ing far a-bove. One of them gave a lit-tle shove, and I fell

gai - ly, glad - ly, mad - ly in - to love. (What should I)

D.S. for Solos & Out Chorus

SUPPLEMENTAL MATERIAL - This Happy Madness

Performance Note: This tune is often performed as a medium bossa, e.g.

(etc.)

Scales for Soloing (for chords with alterations)

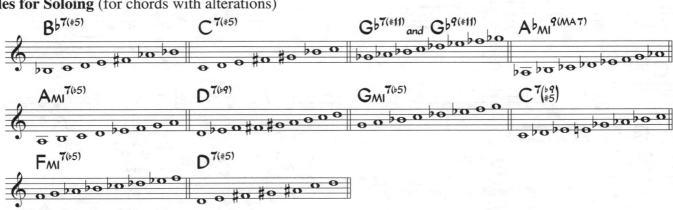

Sample Piano Voicings

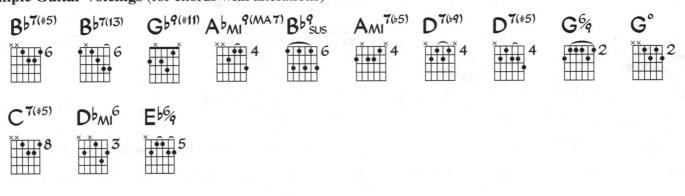

Sample Guitar Voicings (for chords with alterations)

Tin Tin Deo

Music by Walter "Gil" Fuller
Lyric by Chano Pozo
(as recorded by Dizzy Gillespie)

Solo on Tune (A A B C)
After solos, D.S. al Coda
(for D.S.) (or go straight to Coda after solos)

Rhythm hits (letter B) may be ignored for solos.

SUPPLEMENTAL MATERIAL - Tin Tin Deo

Scales for Soloing

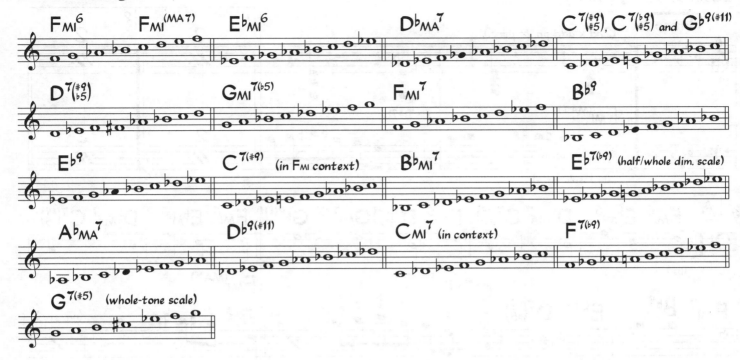

Sample Piano Voicings

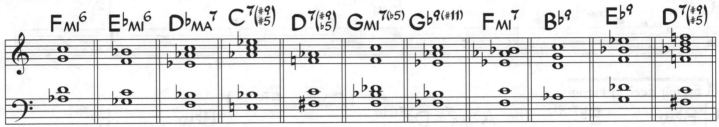

Sample Guitar Voicings (for chords with alterations)

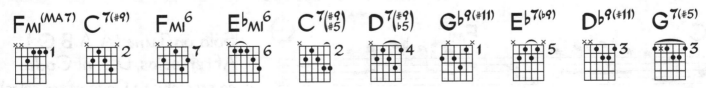

Tin Tin Deo (rhythm section)

SUPPLEMENTAL MATERIAL - Tin Tin Deo

Scales for Soloing

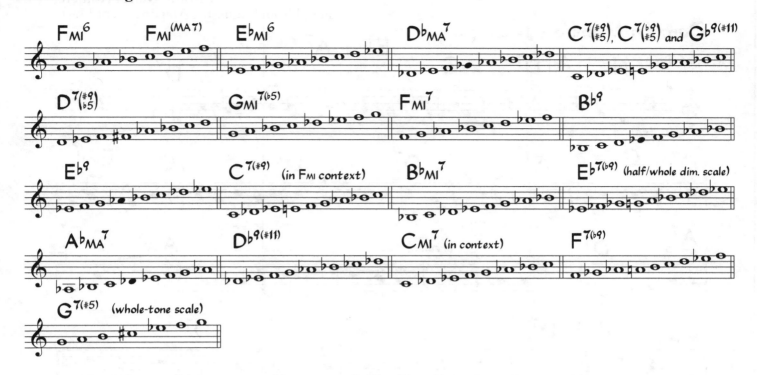

Sample Piano Voicings

Sample Guitar Voicings (for chords with alterations)

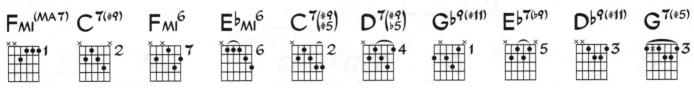

Tres Lindas Cubanas

Guillermo Castillo
Antonio Maria Romeu
(adapted from Orquestra Aragón's recording)

SUPPLEMENTAL MATERIAL - Tres Lindas Cubanas

Scales for Soloing

Note: These scales are identical, except for the "avoid" notes.
The pivotal changes are:
1. G (G) to F# (D⁷) to G (G)
2. B (G) to C (D⁷) to B (G)

Sample Piano Voicings

Sample Bass

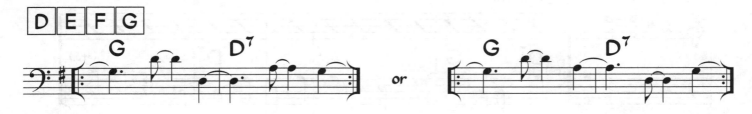

or

Sample Guitar Voicings (for chords with alterations)

Tres Lindas Cubanas (rhythm section)

SUPPLEMENTAL MATERIAL - Tres Lindas Cubanas

Scales for Soloing

Note: These scales are identical, except for the "avoid" notes.

The pivotal changes are:

1. G (G) to F# (D⁷) to G (G)

2. B (G) to C (D⁷) to B (G)

Sample Piano Voicings

Sample Bass

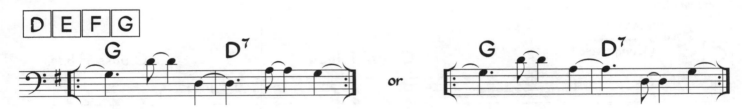

Sample Guitar Voicings (for chords with alterations)

Tumbao

Cal Tjader

(adapted from several Cal Tjader recordings)

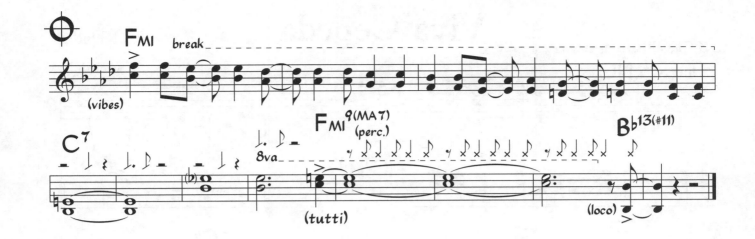

SUPPLEMENTAL MATERIAL - Tumbao

Scales for Soloing (in context)

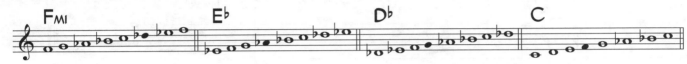

Sample Piano Voicings

Sample Bass (at Letter B)

Sample Percussion   (cowbell pattern during conga solo)

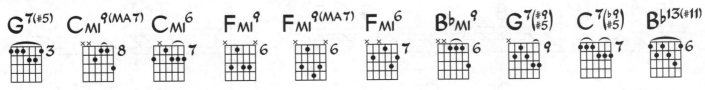

Sample Guitar Voicings (for chords with alterations)

Viva Cepeda

SUPPLEMENTAL MATERIAL - Viva Cepeda

Scales for Soloing

Sample Piano Voicings

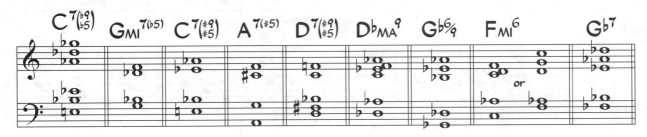

Sample Bass

Sample Guitar Voicings (for chords with alterations)

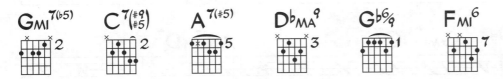

Viva Cepeda (rhythm section)

SUPPLEMENTAL MATERIAL - Viva Cepeda

Scales for Soloing (in F minor context for Letter C)

Sample Piano Voicings

Sample Bass

Sample Guitar Voicings (for chords with alterations)

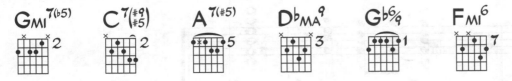

Yuca Con Mojo

(2-3 Clave) Guaracha (♩ = 185)

Rebeca Mauleón

Based on the chord changes of "Picadillo."

SUPPLEMENTAL MATERIAL - Yuca Con Mojo

Scales for Soloing

Sample Piano Montunos

Sample Bass

Sample Guitar Voicings (for chords with alterations)

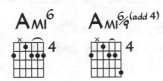

Zina's Zamba

Pete Escovedo

Solo on B C¹ B C², after each solo, play Interlude (D)
After last solo and Interlude, D.S. al Coda (omit 1st ending)

Note: On recording, letter C is repeated (with 2nd ending) before taking Coda.

SUPPLEMENTAL MATERIAL - Zina's Zamba

Scales for Soloing

Sample Piano Voicings

Sample Bass

Sample Guitar Comp for Intro

Sample Guitar Voicings (for chords with alterations)

Photo©Ayano Hisa

CUBAN MUSIC STUDENTS

PART 2:
MORE ADVANCED TUNES

Acrobata

Originally written with the Intro and letter B (with pickups) one octave higher.
This would be suitable for guitar playing the melody.

Solo on Tune (A¹ A² B)
After solos, D.S. al Fine
(w/ repeat)

114

SUPPLEMENTAL MATERIAL - Acrobata

Scales for Soloing

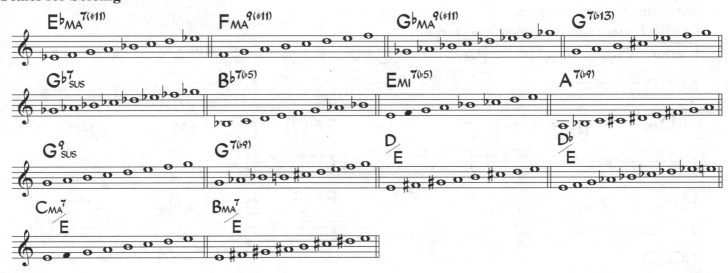

Sample Piano Voicings

Sample Bass

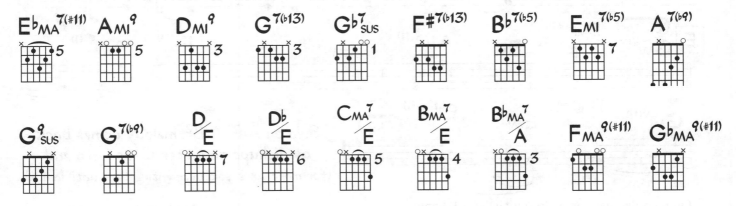

Sample Guitar Voicings (for chords with alterations)

Ao Vento (The Wind)

Music by Chico Pinheiro
Lyric by Guile Wisnik & Paulo Neves

Solo on A B¹ A B², melody comes back
at pickups to letter C, as is to end
(for more solos, solo over entire tune until last x)

On recorded version, solo (guitar) is A B² only.

116

SUPPLEMENTAL MATERIAL - Ao Vento

Scales for Soloing (for chords with alterations)

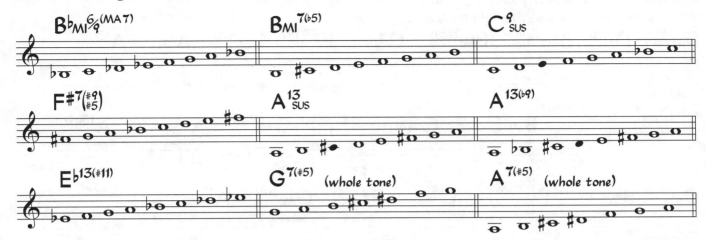

Sample Piano Voicings

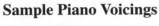

Sample Piano Comp

To letter A

Lyric

(Letters A & B, 1st x)
Um andar tão incerto
Ter o chão todo aberto
Vibração solta no ar
Atento Ao vento

(Letters A & B, 2nd x)
Vendaval sem abrigo
Procurar os amigos
Tudo quer nos apressar
Mas também é preciso dar
Alento Ao tempo

(Letter C)
E o que querem dizer
Carros no ar
Ponte sem mar
Rostos na multidão
Onde vão?

(Letter D)
Mil faróis, mil perigos
Um andar no escuro
Os ruídos noturnos
Da cidade no coração
Atento Ao vento

Ao Vento (rhythm section)

SUPPLEMENTAL MATERIAL - Ao Vento

Scales for Soloing (for chords with alterations)

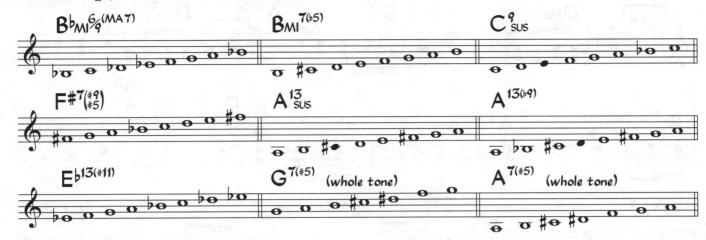

Sample Piano Voicings

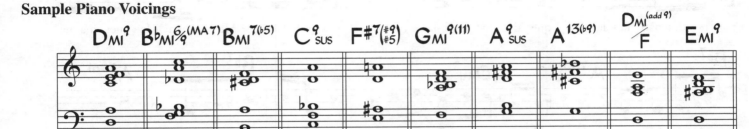

Sample Piano at Letter B

Sample Guitar Voicings (for chords with alterations)

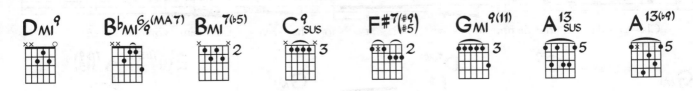

Asa

120

C (3 x's)

D♭I⁹(¹¹)   B♭⁹(¹³)

há pra fa - lar   On - de le - va es - sa la - dei - ra?___ Que

G♭I⁹   1. B♭⁹(¹³)   A⁷(♯⁹♯⁵)

tris - tes ter - ras ven - ce - rá   Um in - ter - pré - te to - can - do Blues?___ Que

2. B♭⁹(¹³)   A⁷(♯⁹♯⁵)   3. B♭⁹(¹³)   A⁷(♯⁹♯⁵)

Um in - tér - pre - te in - ven - tan - do Blues?___ Que Um in - tér - pre - te de - li - ran - do no Blues?___

D (Solos) | till cue | on cue (last x)
D♭I⁹(¹¹) | B♭⁹(¹³) A⁷(♯⁵) | B♭⁹(¹³) A⁷(♯⁵)

                                     Diz que

D.S. (w/ all repeats)
Vamp, solo & fade out
on letter D

SUPPLEMENTAL MATERIAL - Asa

Scales for Soloing

D♭I⁹(¹¹)   B♭⁹(¹³) (with D♭I tonic)   A⁷(♯⁵)

Sample Piano Voicings

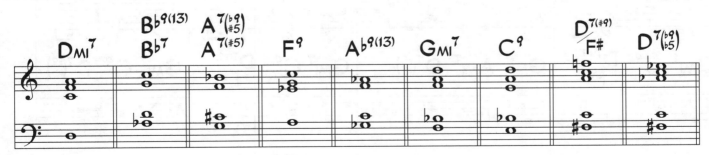

D♭I⁷   B♭⁹(¹³) A⁷(♭⁹♯⁵) F⁹   A♭⁹(¹³) G♭I⁷   C⁹   D⁷(♯⁹)/F♯   D⁷(♭⁹♭⁵)
       B♭⁷   A⁷(♯⁵)

A♭I⁷   D⁷(♭⁹♯⁵) E♭I⁷(♭⁵) D♭I⁹(¹¹) G♭I⁹   A⁷(♯⁹♯⁵)

121

Asa (rhythm section)

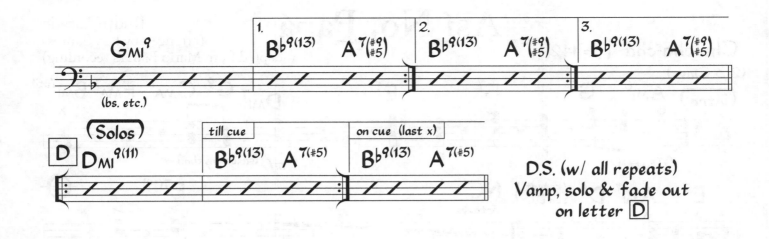

D.S. (w/ all repeats)
Vamp, solo & fade out
on letter D

SUPPLEMENTAL MATERIAL - Asa

Scales for Soloing

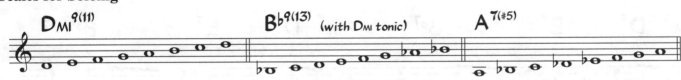

Sample Piano Voicings

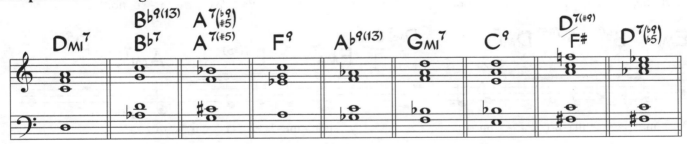

Sample Guitar Voicings (for chords with alterations)

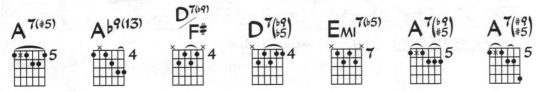

Así No, Papá

Rudy Calzado
(arranged by Ray Santos)
(adapted from Mario Bauza's recording)

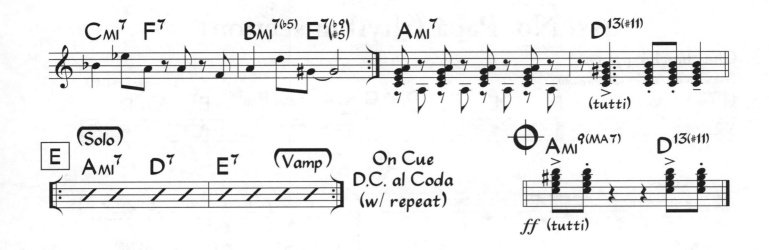

SUPPLEMENTAL MATERIAL - Así No, Papá

Scales for Soloing

Note: Ami7 and D7 have the same scale notes (with G as an "avoid" note for D7). A good thing to stress going from Ami7 to D7 is G to F#. In the E7 scale, G# is a very important "defining" note. So, pivotal notes to perhaps stress in playing through the pattern are G (for Ami7) to F# (for D7) to G# (for E7).

Sample Piano Voicings

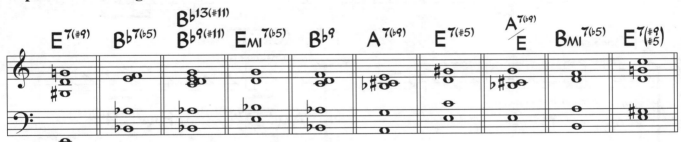

Extra Lyrics

Verse 2 (Letter A, 2nd x)
> Así no, mi cariñito, no ves que me vuelvo loca.
> Que si lo bailas bonito el cuerpo se me alborota.

Verse 3 (Letter A, 3rd x)
> Ven acá, mi papacito, que la cosa está en candela,
> porqué de la guardia vieja es mi sabroso soncito.

Así No, Papá (rhythm section)

SUPPLEMENTAL MATERIAL - Así No, Papá

Scales for Soloing

Sample Piano Voicings

Alternate Piano Montunos

(both hands)

Alternate Bass Tumbao

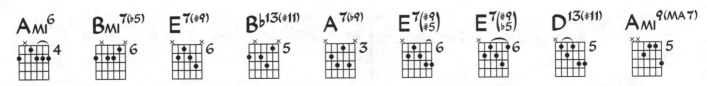

Sample Guitar Voicings (for chords with alterations)

Ami⁶   Bmi⁷⁽ᵇ⁵⁾   E⁷⁽♯⁹⁾   B♭¹³⁽♯¹¹⁾   A⁷⁽ᵇ⁹⁾   E⁷⁽♯⁹♯⁵⁾   E⁷⁽♯⁹ᵇ⁵⁾   D¹³⁽♯¹¹⁾   Ami⁹⁽ᴹᴬ⁷⁾

Así No, Papá (horns, background)

SUPPLEMENTAL MATERIAL - Así No, Papá

Scales for Soloing

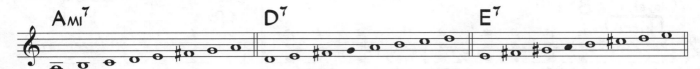

Azulito

Ray Santos
(adapted from Mario Bauza's recording)

SUPPLEMENTAL MATERIAL - Azulito

Scale for Soloing (for chords with alterations)

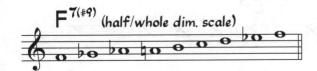

Sample Guitar Voicings (for chords with alterations)

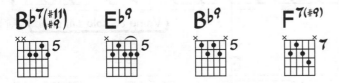

Azulito (rhythm section)

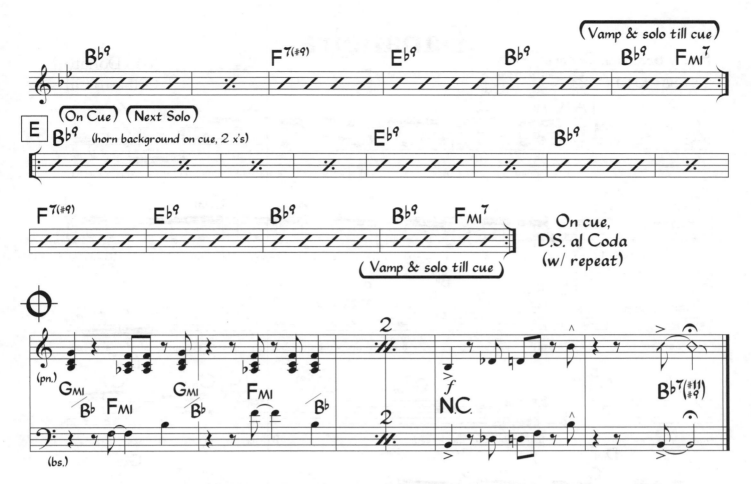

SUPPLEMENTAL MATERIAL - Azulito

Sample Piano Voicings

Scale for Soloing (for chords with alterations)

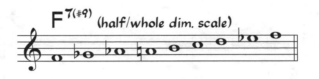

Sample Bass

Bananeira

This chart takes aspects from several different versions.

SUPPLEMENTAL MATERIAL - Bananeira

Scales for Soloing

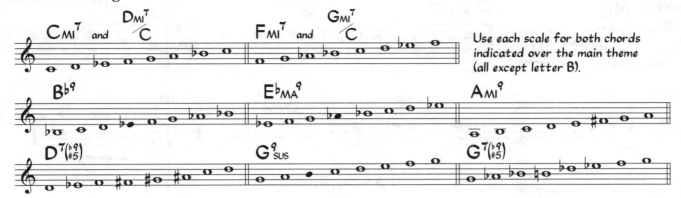

Use each scale for both chords indicated over the main theme (all except letter B).

Sample Piano Voicings

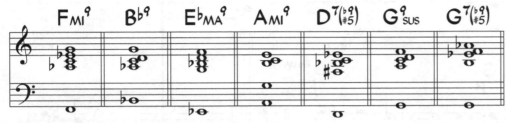

Sample Piano Comping (except for letter B)

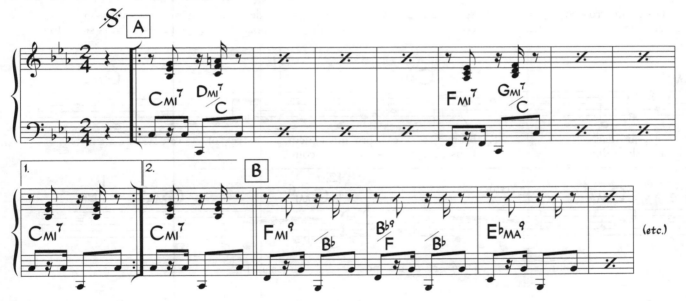

(etc.)

Sample Bass

(etc.)

Sample Guitar Voicings (for chords with alterations)

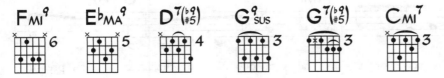

-ro mor-rer_____ a____ dar ou-vi-do ce-leu - ma_e lhe per - der.

Repeat to letter A

Não me dei - xe sem me ou -

D.S. al Coda (w/ all repeats)

- re-sol - ver._____ (instrumental)

Solos may be played on A¹ A² B A³ before taking the D.S.

SUPPLEMENTAL MATERIAL - Celeuma

Scales for Soloing (for chords with alterations)

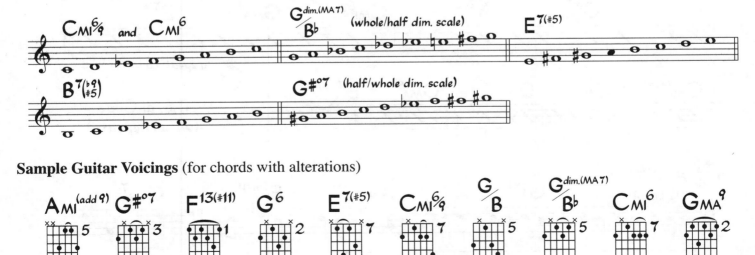

Sample Guitar Voicings (for chords with alterations)

Celeuma (rhythm section)

Solos may be played on A[1] A[2] B A[3] before taking the D.S.

SUPPLEMENTAL MATERIAL - Celeuma

Scales for Soloing (for chords with alterations)

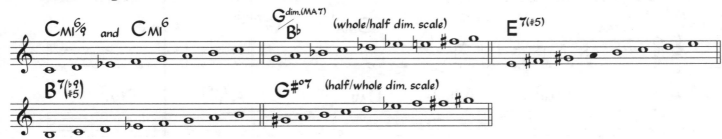

Sample Piano Voicings

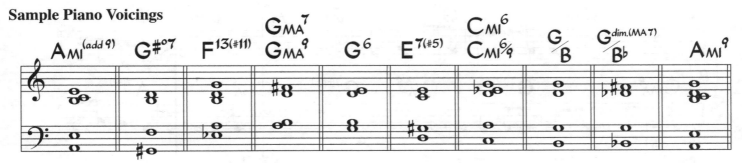

Sample Bass

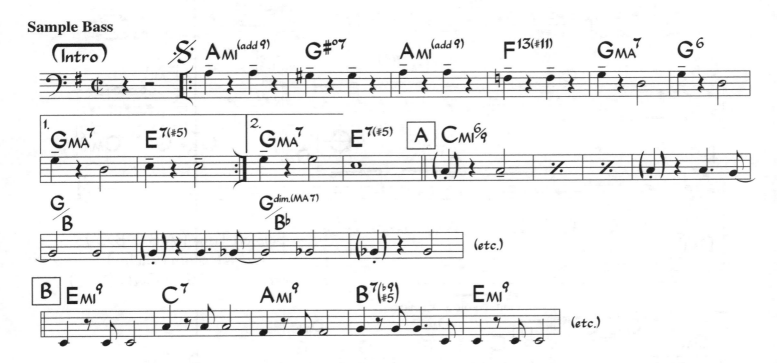

(etc.)

(etc.)

Sample Guitar Voicings (for chords with alterations)

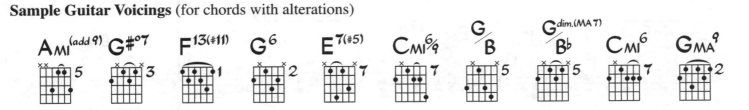

Chakalaka

Andy Narell

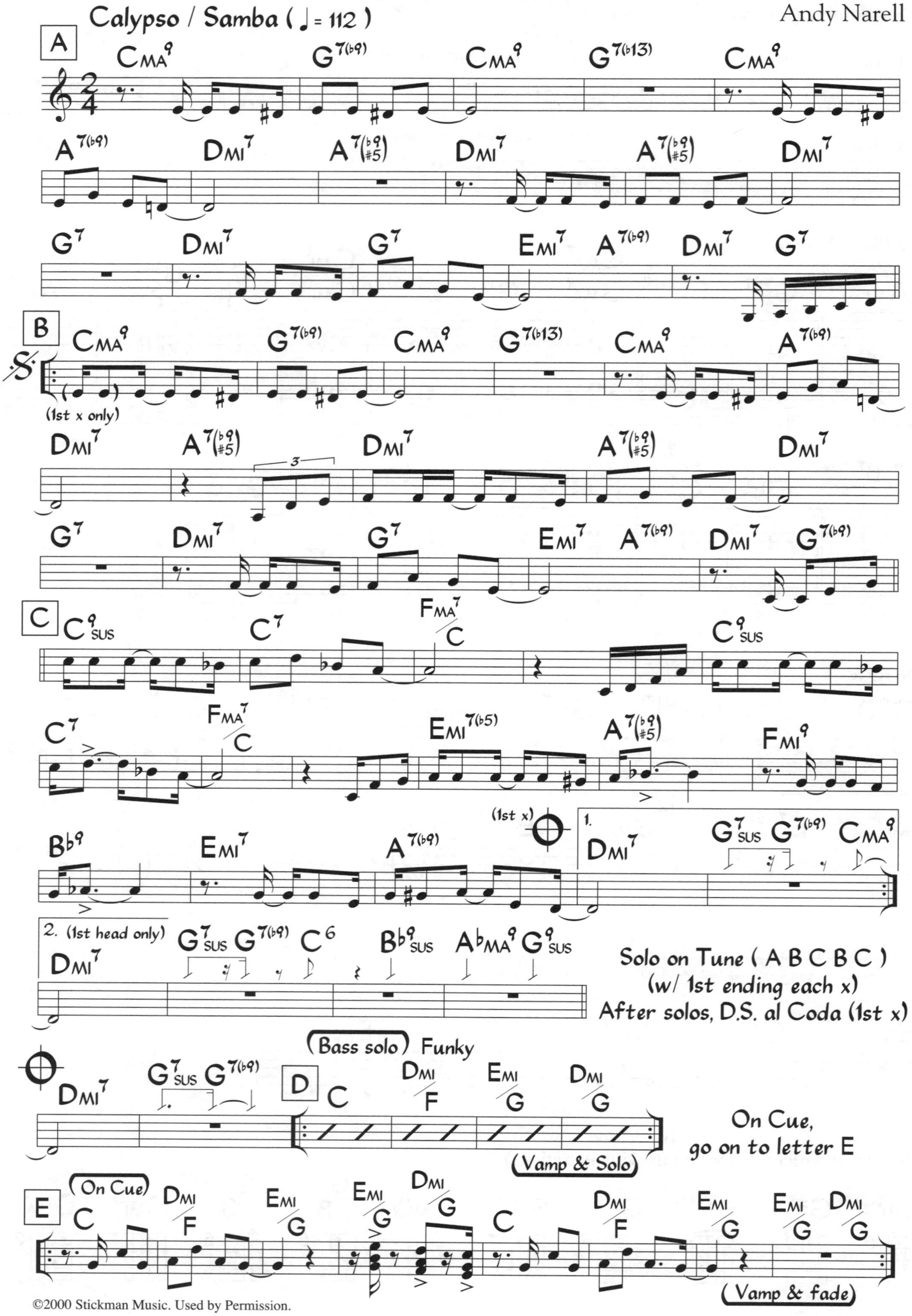

SUPPLEMENTAL MATERIAL - Chakalaka

Scales for Soloing (for chords with alterations)

Sample Piano Voicings

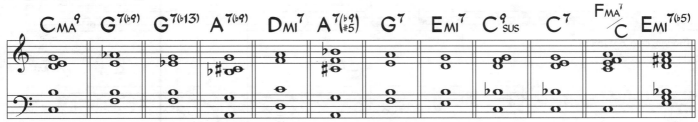

Sample Bass

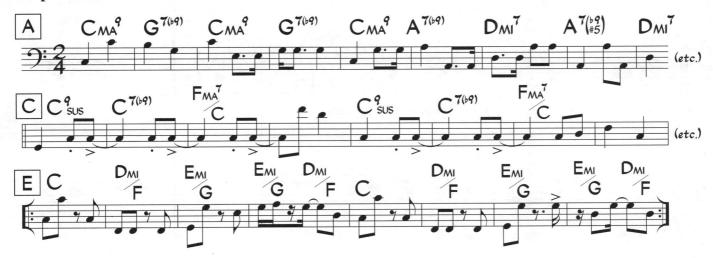

Sample Guitar Voicings (for chords with alterations)

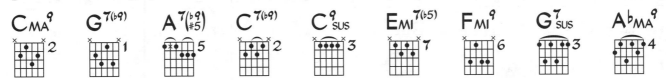

Congo Yambumba

SUPPLEMENTAL MATERIAL - Congo Yambumba

Scales for Soloing

Sample Guitar Voicings (for chords with alterations)

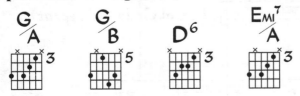

Congo Yambumba (rhythm section)

SUPPLEMENTAL MATERIAL - Congo Yambumba

Scales for Soloing

Sample Guitar Voicings (for chords with alterations)

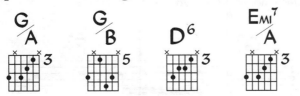

Dia Azul

or por te que-rer.＿ Vi-ver é mais do que sa-ir sal-van-do o que po-de,

e com a-mor a vi-da ex-plo-de.

D.S. al Coda (w/ repeat)
(solo until pickups to B)

a vi-da ex-plo-de.＿＿

SUPPLEMENTAL MATERIAL - Dia Azul

Scales for Soloing (for chords with alterations)

Sample Piano Voicings

Sample Bass (& comp rhythm)

(or this type of guitar comp)

Sample Guitar Voicings (for chords with alterations)

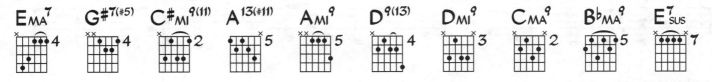

El Marelito

After solos, D.C. al Fine w/ all repeats
(A A B A A Coda to Fine)

Opt. back to letter D for more solos

SUPPLEMENTAL MATERIAL - El Marelito

Scales for Soloing

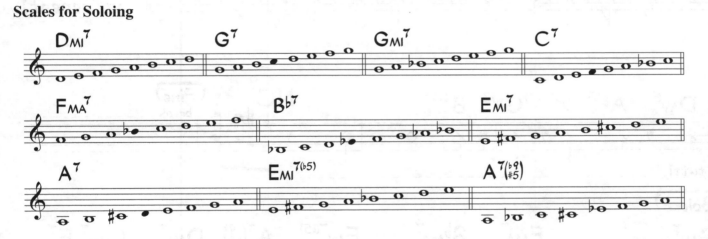

El Marelito (rhythm section)

G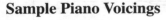

Opt. back to letter D for more solos

(tutti)

After solos, D.C. al Fine w/ all repeats
(A A B A A Coda to Fine)

SUPPLEMENTAL MATERIAL - El Marelito

Sample Piano Voicings

Sample Piano Montuno

Sample Bass

Sample Guitar Voicings (for chords with alterations)

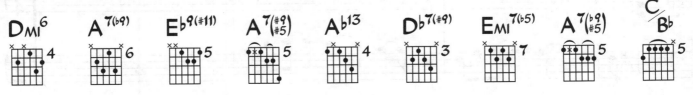

Fuji

Cal Tjader

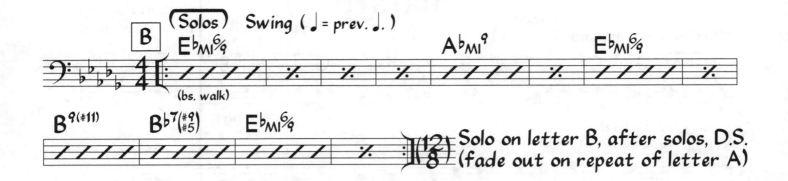

SUPPLEMENTAL MATERIAL - Fuji

Scales for Soloing

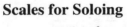

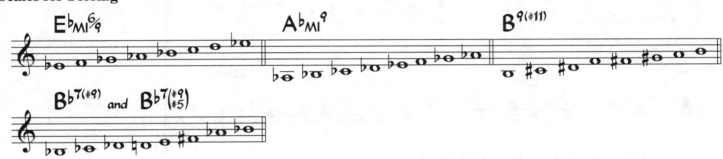

Sample Piano Voicings

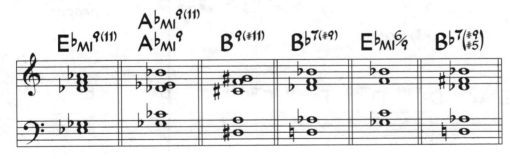

Sample Guitar Voicings (for chords with alterations)

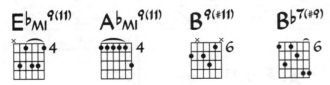

153

Guararé

Juan Formell
(adapted from Ray Barretto's recording)

SUPPLEMENTAL MATERIAL - Guararé

Scales for Soloing

Sample Guitar Voicings (for chords with alterations)

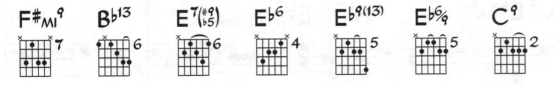

Guararé (horns)

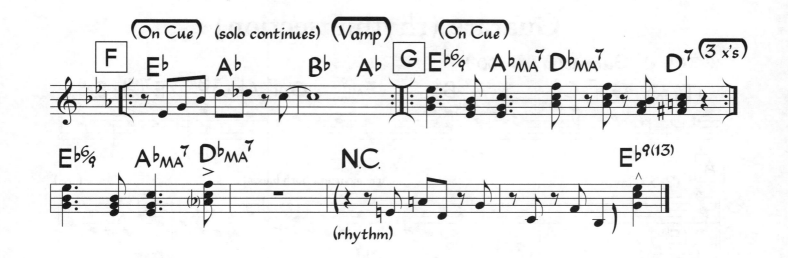

SUPPLEMENTAL MATERIAL - Guararé

Scales for Soloing

Sample Guitar Voicings (for chords with alterations)

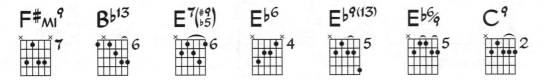

Guararé (rhythm section)

SUPPLEMENTAL MATERIAL - Guararé

Scales for Soloing

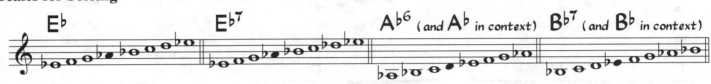

Sample Piano Voicings

Sample Piano Montunos

Havana

Ron Stallings
(as recorded by Que Calor)

160

SUPPLEMENTAL MATERIAL - Havana

Lyric on D.S.

Letter B: (The) spell of sultry nights speaks of great beauty to your soul
Magic in her music to enchant the young and old.

Letter C: As waters flow, winds come and go. Her destiny unfolds.
So dry your eyes and tell no lies. Havana is her own.

Letter D: The future's in our hands. The willing strength to understand,
That we all share the Master Plan.
For in Havana, Español Afric Havana.
Where the spirits dance, Havana, waits my love.

Scales for Soloing

Havana (rhythm section)

SUPPLEMENTAL MATERIAL - *Havana*

Scales for Soloing

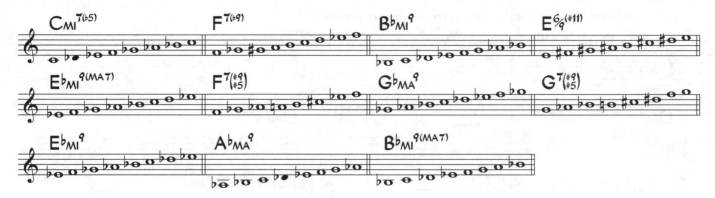

Sample Piano Voicings

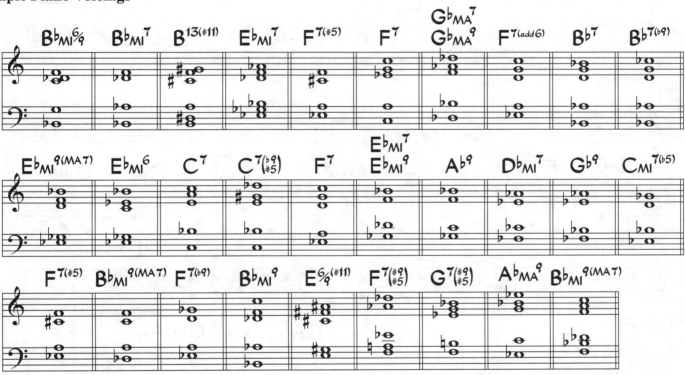

Sample Guitar Voicings (for chords with alterations)

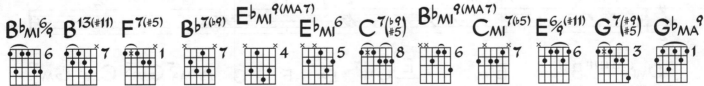

Heart Of Darkness

Medium Cha-cha-chá (♩ = 136)

(Optional Intro: Rhythm Section play letter A without the melody)

Don Grolnick

164

SUPPLEMENTAL MATERIAL - Heart Of Darkness

Scales for Soloing

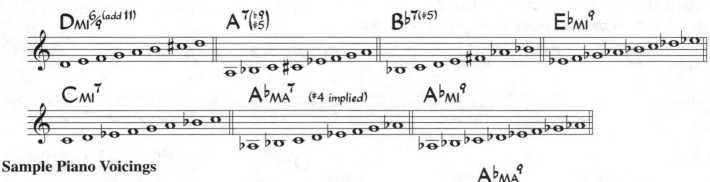

Sample Piano Voicings

(left-hand voicings for solos)

Sample Bass

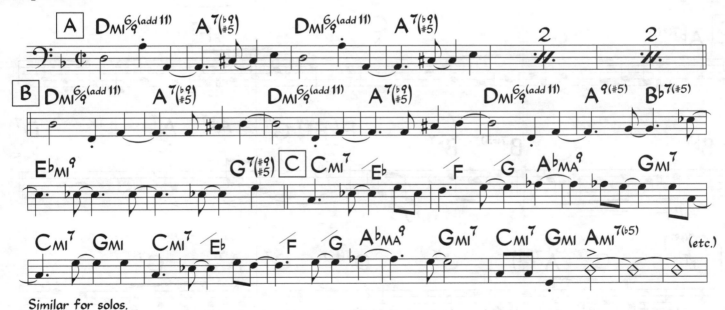

Similar for solos.

Sample Guitar Voicings (for chords with alterations)

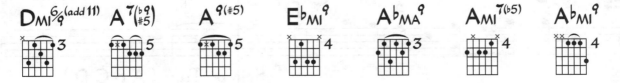

Hey, Bud

David Torres
(adapted from Poncho Sanchez' recording)

Medium Cha-cha-chá (♩ = 132)
Intro: Rhythm Section plays bars 1-4 of A 2 x's

Solo on Tune (A B C D)
- or -
Solo on simplified solo changes (page 2)
After solos, D.S. al Coda

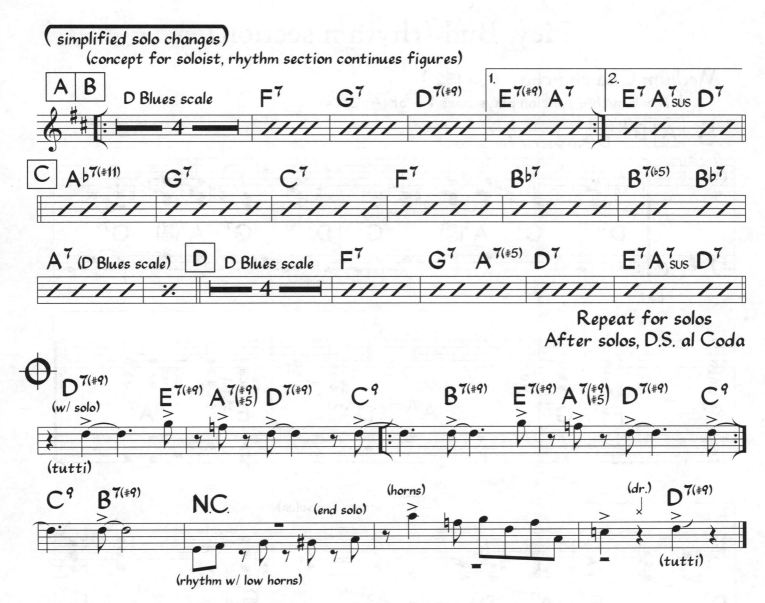

Note: Rhythm figures are played for solos, except anticipation into letter D.

SUPPLEMENTAL MATERIAL - Hey, Bud

Scales for Soloing

Hey, Bud (rhythm section)

Medium Cha-cha-chá (♩ = 132)

Intro: Rhythm Section plays bars 1-4 of [A] 2 x's

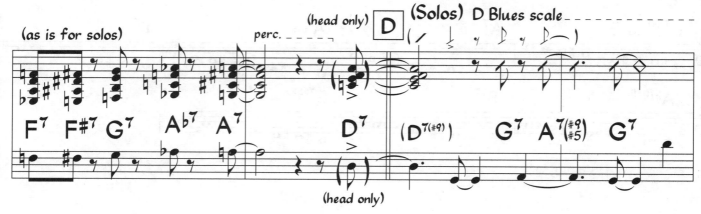

Solo on Tune (A B C D) (changes are
written out separately on other parts)

Play figures during solos
(except the anticipation to letter D)
After solos, D.S. al Coda

Note: The main and background parts are laid out differently from this part.

SUPPLEMENTAL MATERIAL - Hey, Bud

Sample Guitar Voicings (for chords with alterations)

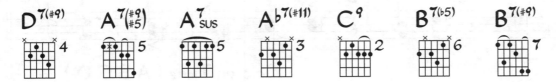

Hey, Bud (horn background parts)

Medium Cha-cha-chá (♩ = 132)
Intro: Rhythm Section plays bars 1-4 of [A] 2 x's

Solo on Tune (A B C D)

\- or -

Solo on simplified solo changes (page 2)

After solos, D.S. al Coda

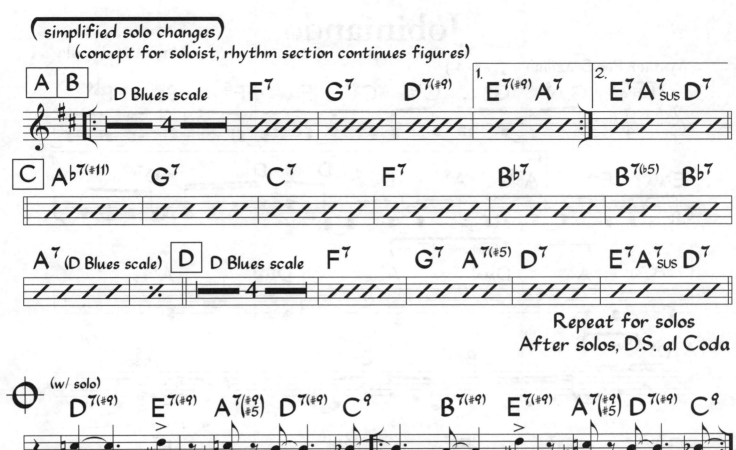

Repeat for solos
After solos, D.S. al Coda

Note: Rhythm figures are played for solos, except anticipation into letter D.

SUPPLEMENTAL MATERIAL - Hey, Bud

Scales for Soloing

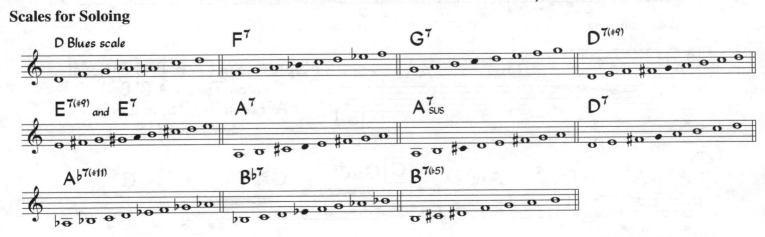

Jobiniando

go - ra vou   te con - tar.___   Cho - rei___ ao to - car___ "Che - ga de___ Sau - da-

- - - - de."___   E se___   meu a - mor___ quer can - tar,___   Eu si-

- go e "Vi - vo so - nhan - - - do."   Jo - bi - ni - an - - - do, "Eu Sei Que

Vamp & fade

Vou___ Te A - mar."___   E se___

SUPPLEMENTAL MATERIAL - Jobiniando

Scales for Soloing

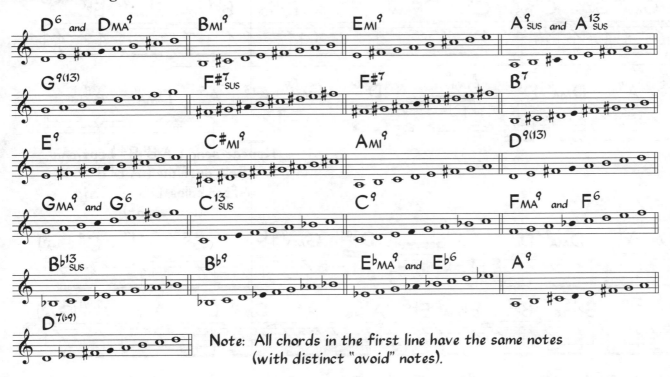

Note: All chords in the first line have the same notes
(with distinct "avoid" notes).

Jobiniando (rhythm section)

SUPPLEMENTAL MATERIAL - Jobiniando

Scales for Soloing

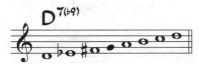

All other scales are without alterations. (See main part.)

Sample Piano Voicings

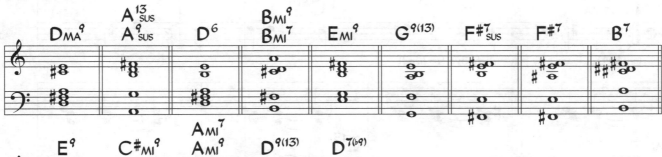

Sample Bass

(etc.)   (similar for Coda)

Sample Guitar Voicings (for chords with alterations)

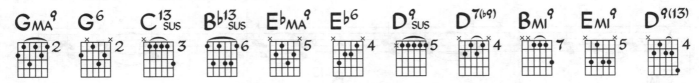

Ladies In Mercedes (main part)

Mellow, jagged "Samba" (♩ = 96-124)

Steve Swallow

Play head 2 x's
Solo on Tune (A B)
After solos,
D.C. al Coda
(no repeat)

SUPPLEMENTAL MATERIAL - Ladies In Mercedes

Scales for Soloing (for chords with alterations)

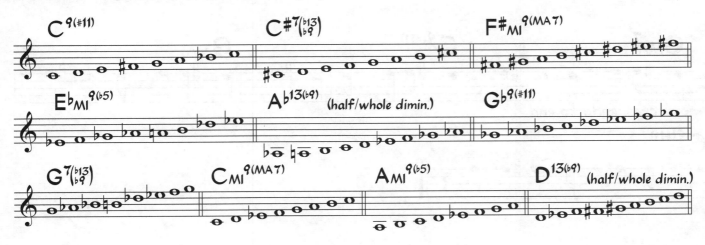

Ladies In Mercedes (melody only)

Mellow, jagged "Samba" (♩ = 96-124)

Play head 2 x's, solo on A B
After solos, D.C. al Coda (no repeat)

crescendo to end

f

SUPPLEMENTAL MATERIAL - Ladies In Mercedes

Scales for Soloing (for chords with alterations)

Sample Bass (for solos)

Sample Guitar Voicings (for chords with alterations)

Mambo Rincón

Ray Santos
(adapted from Mario Bauza's recording)

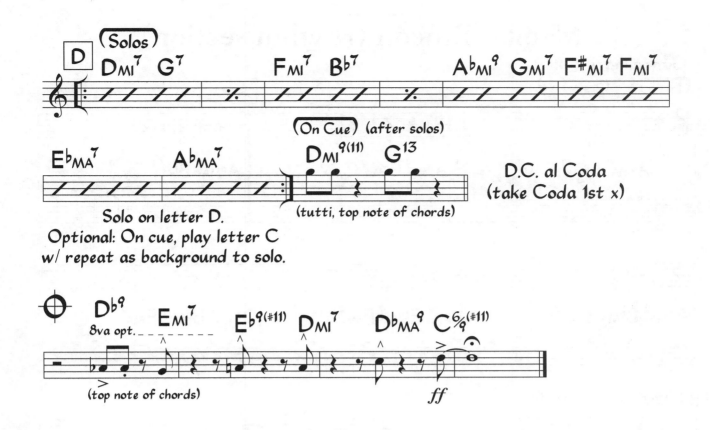

SUPPLEMENTAL MATERIAL - Mambo Rincón

Scales for Soloing

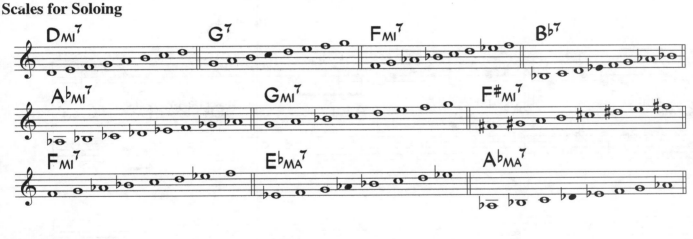

Sample Guitar Voicings (for chords with alterations)

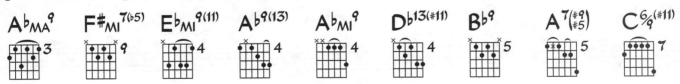

Mambo Rincón (rhythm section)

SUPPLEMENTAL MATERIAL - Mambo Rincón

Sample Piano Voicings

Montuno Blue

SUPPLEMENTAL MATERIAL - Montuno Blue

Scales for Soloing

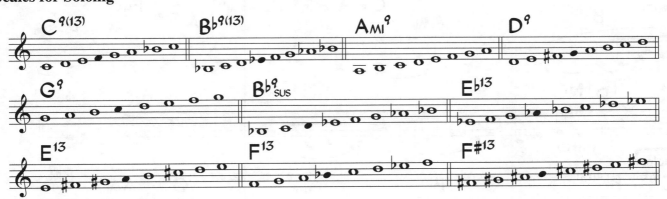

Sample Guitar Voicings (for chords with alterations)

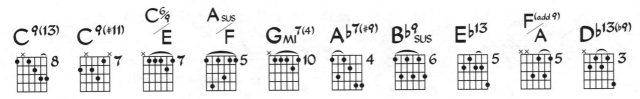

Montuno Blue (harmony part)

Repeat E¹ E² F G for more solos
After last solo, go on to letter H

* "A²" is the 2nd x through a repeated letter A on other parts.

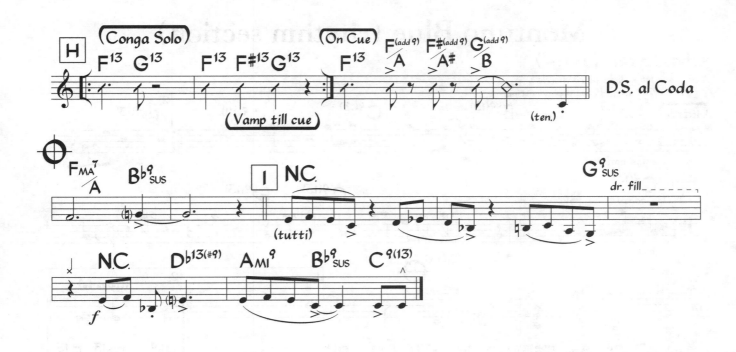

SUPPLEMENTAL MATERIAL - Montuno Blue

Scales for Soloing

Montuno Blue (rhythm section)

Repeat E¹ E² F G for more solos
After last solo, go on to letter H

D.S. al Coda
(w/ repeat)

SUPPLEMENTAL MATERIAL - Montuno Blue

Sample Piano Voicings

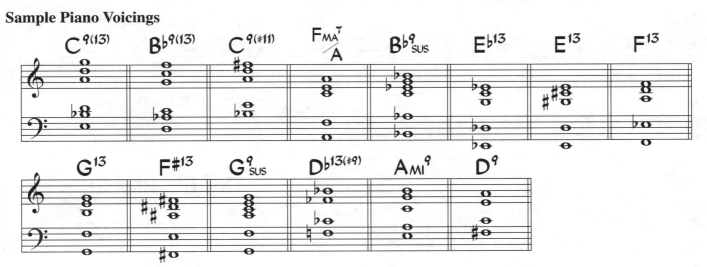

Sample Piano Montuno (at Letter H)

Muñeca

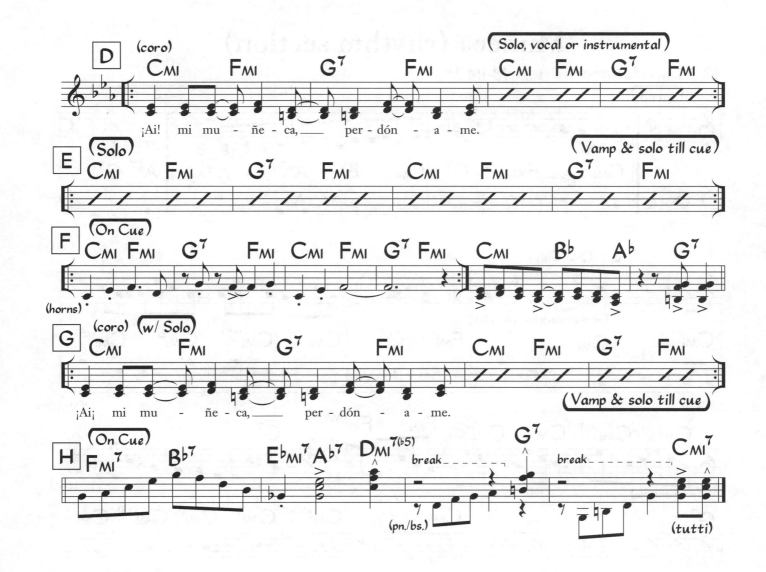

SUPPLEMENTAL MATERIAL - Muñeca

Scales for Soloing

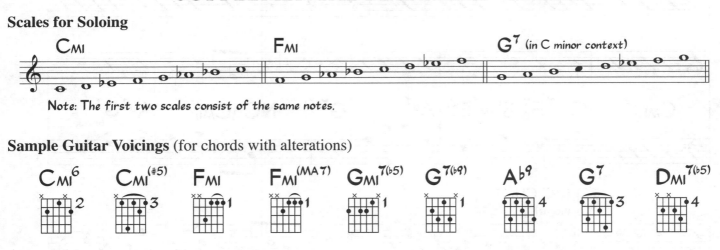

Note: The first two scales consist of the same notes.

Sample Guitar Voicings (for chords with alterations)

Muñeca (rhythm section)

SUPPLEMENTAL MATERIAL - Muñeca

Scales for Soloing

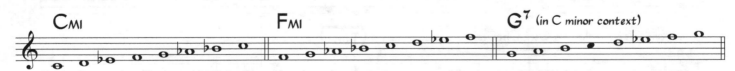

Note: The first two scales consist of the same notes.

Sample Guitar Voicings (for chords with alterations)

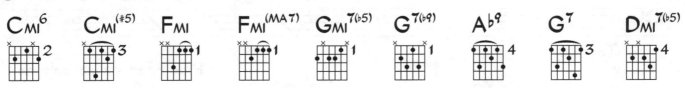

No Borders

Rebeca Mauleón

Play head twice, solo on tune (A B) (omit breaks). After solos, play head 1 x, then D.C., vamp on Intro w/ solo, till Fine on cue.

SUPPLEMENTAL MATERIAL - No Borders

Scales for Soloing

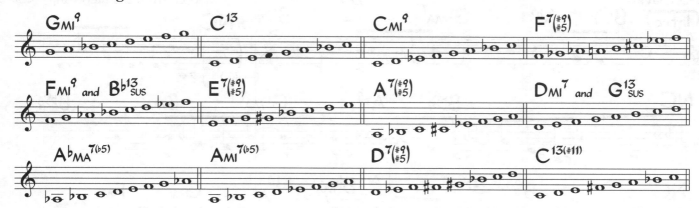

Sample Piano Voicings

Sample Percussion Parts

(suggested cowbell pattern, played on two bells)   (ride cymbal pattern - head and solos)

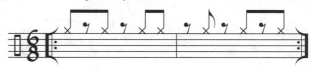

Rhythm Section Notes

- Bass maintains similar feel throughout (like Intro)
- Piano comps freely
- Percussionists can play straight Afro-Cuban 6/8 feel
- Drummer can alternate between Afro-Cuban 6/8 feel for head and solos, and swing at the bridge
  (letter B).

Sample Guitar Voicings (for chords with alterations)

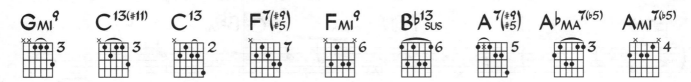

Nunca Contigo

SUPPLEMENTAL MATERIAL - Nunca Contigo

Scales for Soloing

Think C⁷ tonality for both chords.

Sample Guitar Voicings (for chords with alterations)

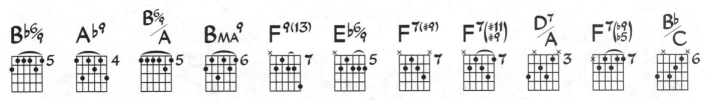

Nunca Contigo (rhythm section)

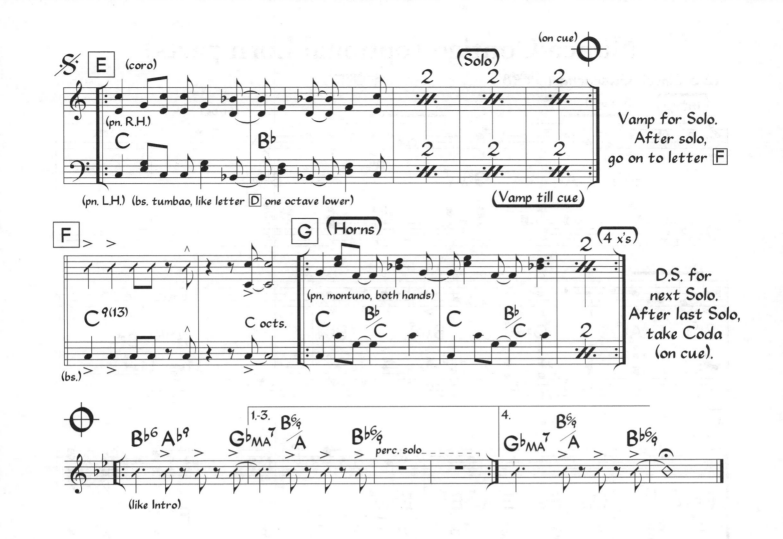

SUPPLEMENTAL MATERIAL - Nunca Contigo

Scales for Soloing

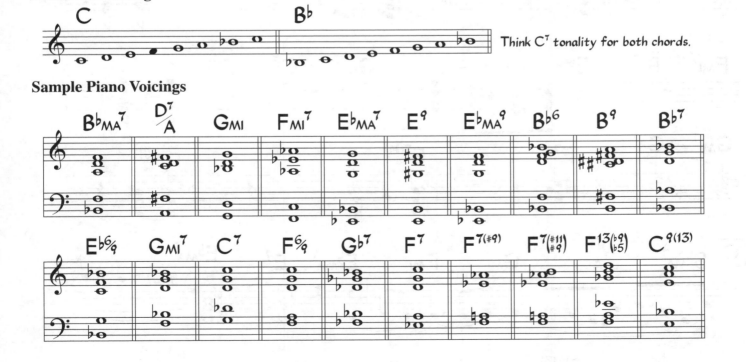

Think C⁷ tonality for both chords.

Sample Piano Voicings

Nunca Contigo (optional horn parts)

SUPPLEMENTAL MATERIAL - Nunca Contigo

Scales for Soloing

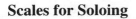

Think C⁷ tonality for both chords.

On A Sunday Afternoon

SUPPLEMENTAL MATERIAL - On A Sunday Afternoon

Scales for Soloing (for chords with alterations)

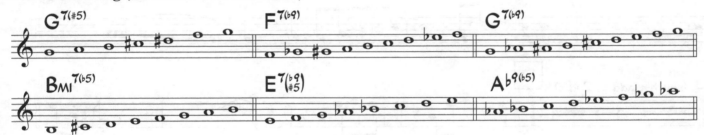

On A Sunday Afternoon (harmony part)

SUPPLEMENTAL MATERIAL - On A Sunday Afternoon

Scales for Soloing (for chords with alterations)

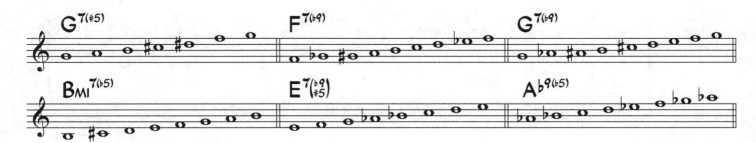

On A Sunday Afternoon (rhythm section)

Scales for Soloing (for chords with alterations)

Sample Piano Voicings

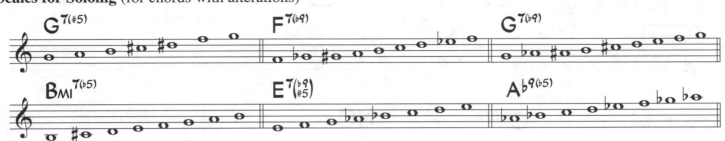

Sample Guitar Voicings (for chords with alterations)

Opita's Opus

Jorge Dalto
(as recorded by Patato Valdez)

©1989 Dalto Music. Used by Permission.

208

SUPPLEMENTAL MATERIAL - Opita's Opus

Scales for Soloing

Sample Piano Voicings

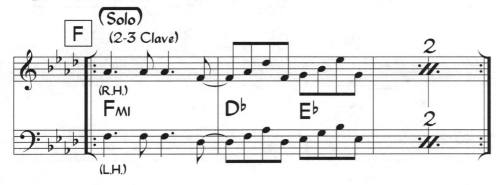

Sample Piano Montuno

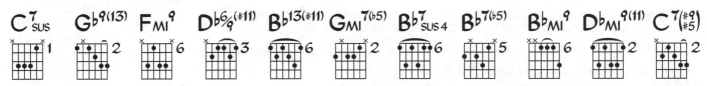

Sample Guitar Voicings (for chords with alterations)

Opita's Opus (rhythm section)

SUPPLEMENTAL MATERIAL - Opita's Opus

Scales for Soloing

Sample Piano Voicings

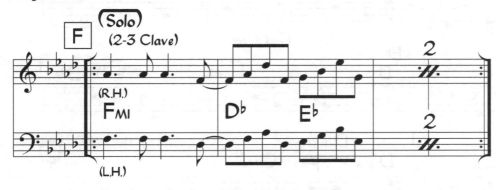

Sample Piano Montuno

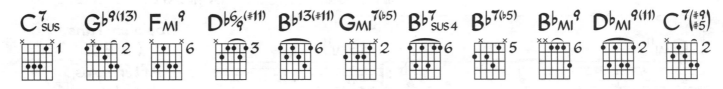

Sample Guitar Voicings (for chords with alterations)

C7SUS   Gb9(13)   FMI9   Db6/9(#11)   Bb13(#11)   GMI7(b5)   Bb7SUS4   Bb7(b5)   BbMI9   DbMI9(11)   C7(#9/#5)

Partido Alto

During solos, anticipations in letter B and rhythm figures in letter B, measures 4 and 12 are played.

212

SUPPLEMENTAL MATERIAL - Partido Alto

Scales for Soloing

Sample Piano Voicings

Sample comp for Intro and (optional) for solos

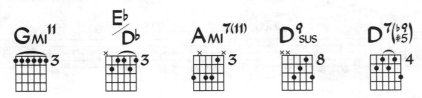

Sample Guitar Voicings (for chords with alterations)

Partido Alto (bass part)

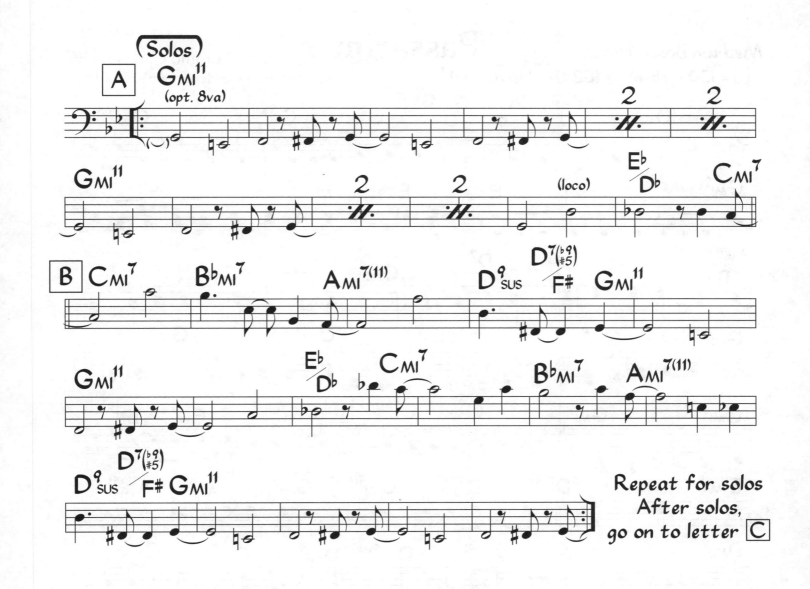

SUPPLEMENTAL MATERIAL - Partido Alto

Scales for Soloing

Passarim

Medium Bossa Nova
(♩ = 130 (Jobim) ♩ = 162 (Joe Henderson))

Antonio Carlos Jobim
(adapted from Joe Henderson's recording)

©1985 Corcovado Music. Used by Permission.

216

SUPPLEMENTAL MATERIAL - *Passarim*

Scales for Soloing

Sample Piano Voicings

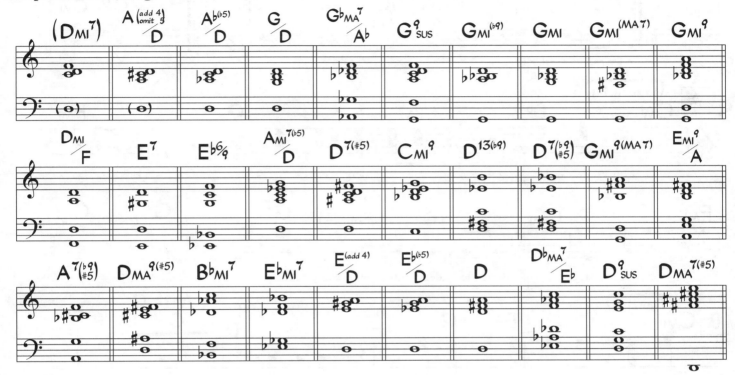

Sample Bass

Sample Guitar Voicings (for chords with alterations)

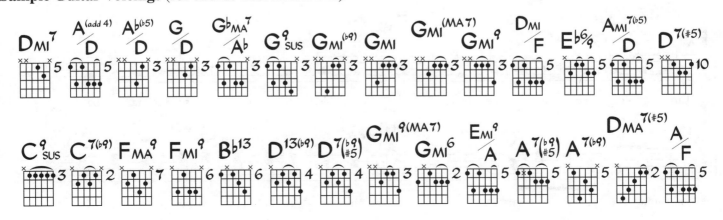

Que Le Den Candela

Rodolfo C. Cardenas
(arranged by J.P. Torres)
(adapted from Descarga Boricua's recording)

SUPPLEMENTAL MATERIAL - Que Le Den Candela

Scales for Soloing

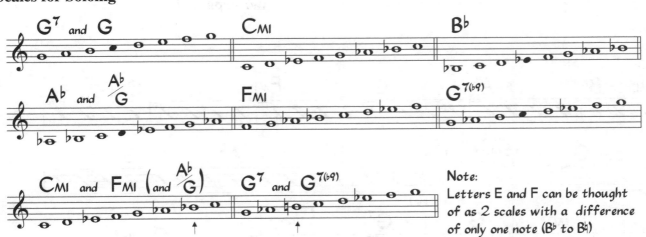

Note:
Letters E and F can be thought of as 2 scales with a difference of only one note (B♭ to B♮)

Que Le Den Candela (rhythm section)

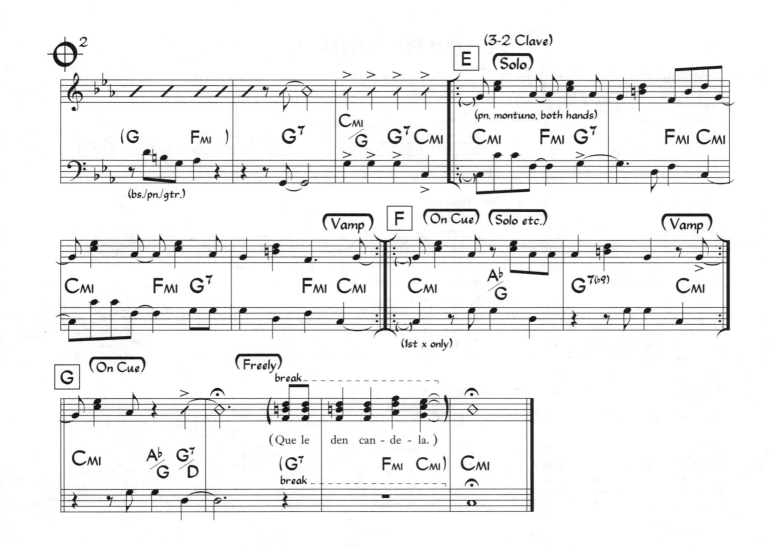

SUPPLEMENTAL MATERIAL - Que Le Den Candela

Scales for Soloing

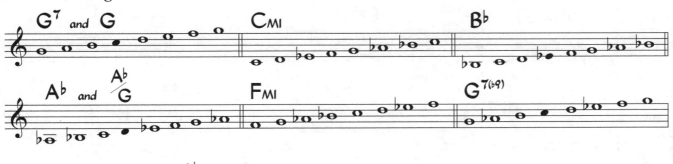

Note:
Letters E and F can be thought
of as 2 scales with a difference
of only one note (B♭ to B♮)

Sample Guitar Voicings (for chords with alterations)

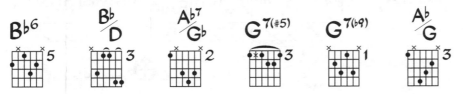

Renata Maria

Music by Ivan Lins
Lyric by Chico Buarque
(as recorded by Ivan Lins)

Note: Ivan Lins sings this song in the key of C.
It is transposed to E♭ to make it more easily playable by instrumentalists.

SUPPLEMENTAL MATERIAL - Renata Maria

Selected Scales for Soloing

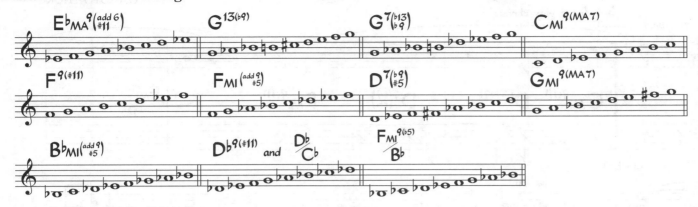

Selected Sample Piano Voicings

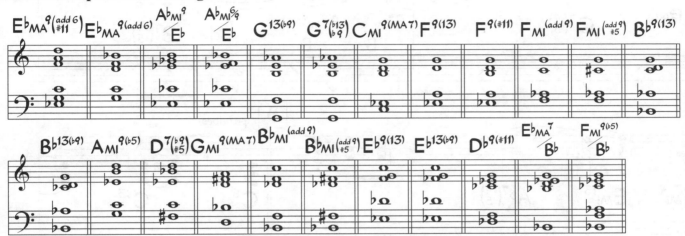

Sample Bass

Sample Guitar (continue through tune)

Sample Guitar Voicings (for chords with alterations)

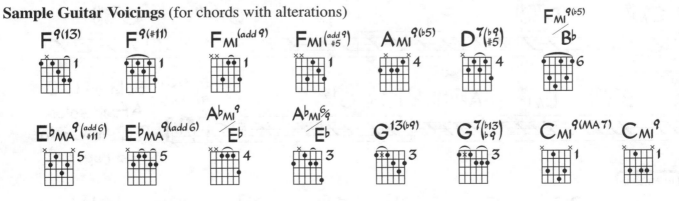

Extra Lyric (for letters A, A and B, 2nd x)

Dia após dia, na praia, com olhos vazados de já não a ver,
Quieto como um pescadpr a juntar seus anzóis
Ou como algum salva-vidas no banco dos réus.
Noite na ptaia deserta, deserta daquela mulher
Praia repleta de rastros em mil direçóes.

Penso que todos os passos perdidos são meus.
Eu já sabia, meu Deus, tão fulgurante visão
Não se produz duas vezes num mesmo lugar.
Mas que danado fui eu enquanto Renata Maria
saía do mar.

Rojo Y Negro

SUPPLEMENTAL MATERIAL - Rojo Y Negro

Scales for Soloing

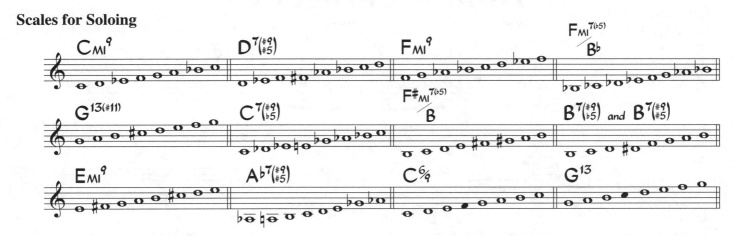

Sample Piano Voicings

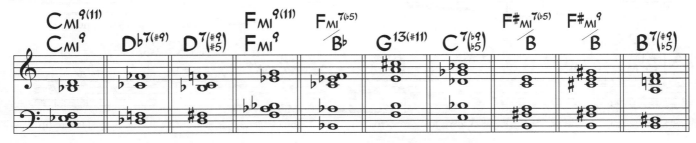

Sample Bass (for solos)

Sample Guitar Voicings (for chords with alterations)

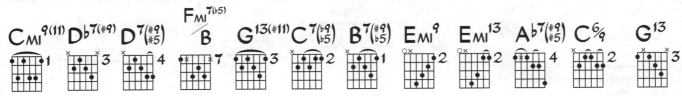

Rompe Saragüey

Son-Montuno (♩ = 130)
(2-3 Clave)

Virgilio Gonzalez
(adapted from Hector Lavoe's recording)

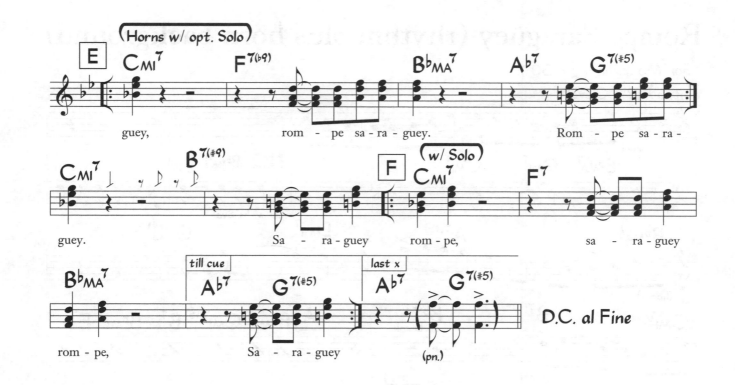

SUPPLEMENTAL MATERIAL - Rompe Saragüey

Scales for Soloing

Consider C$_{MI}$^{7} and F^7 (in solos) as closely related.

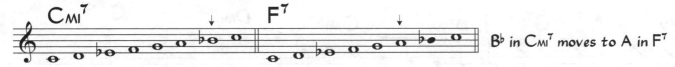

B♭ in C$_{MI}$^{7} moves to A in F^7

Sample Guitar Voicings (for chords with alterations)

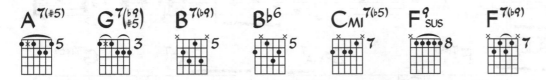

227

Rompe Saragüey (rhythm plus horn background)

SUPPLEMENTAL MATERIAL - Rompe Saragüey

Scales for Soloing

Consider CMI⁷ and F⁷ (in solos) as closely related.

B♭ in CMI⁷ moves to A in F⁷

Sample Piano Voicings

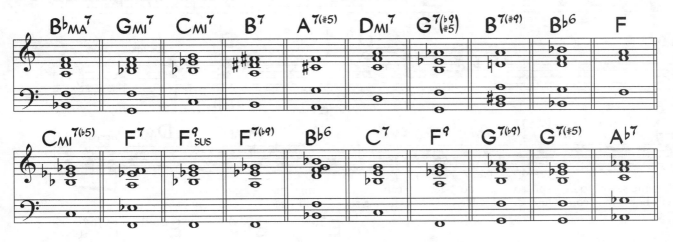

Sample Piano Montuno (for solos)

Sample Bass

SUPPLEMENTAL MATERIAL - Sabroso Guaguancó

Scales for Soloing

only differences are G to G#
and "avoid" note A over E⁷

scales are identical except
for "avoid" note A on E⁷

Sample Guitar Voicings (for chords with alterations)

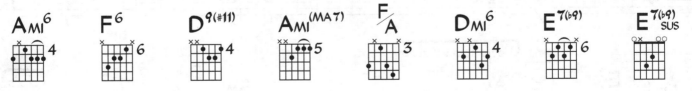

Sabroso Guaguancó (rhythm section)

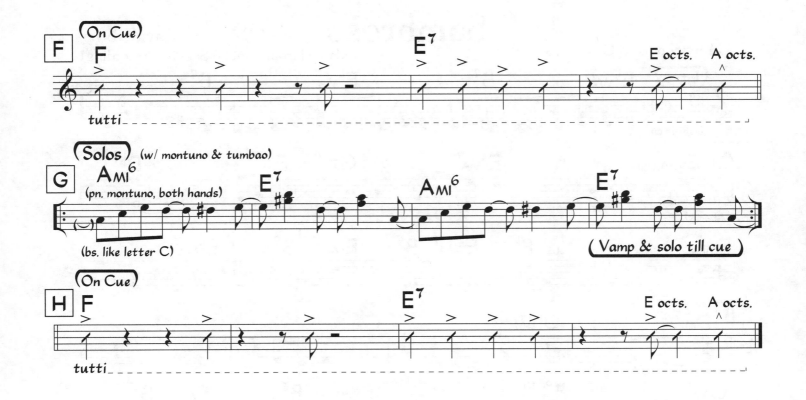

SUPPLEMENTAL MATERIAL - Sabroso Guaguancó

Scales for Soloing

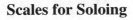

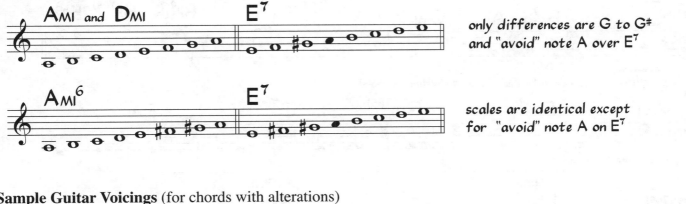

only differences are G to G♯ and "avoid" note A over E⁷

scales are identical except for "avoid" note A on E⁷

Sample Guitar Voicings (for chords with alterations)

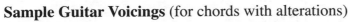

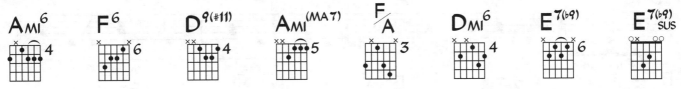

Sambroso

David Torres
(adapted from Poncho Sanchez' recording)

234

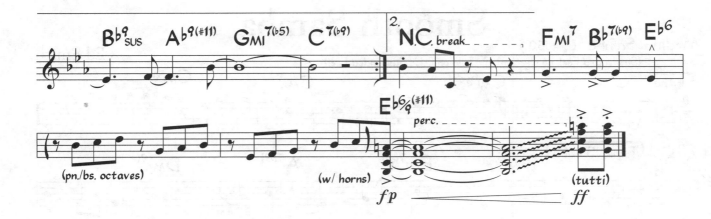

SUPPLEMENTAL MATERIAL - Sambroso

Scales for Soloing (for chords with alterations)

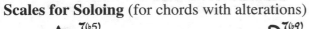

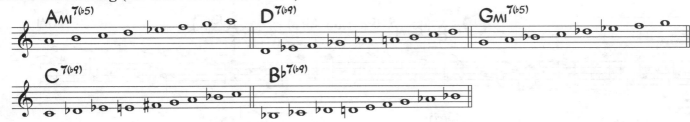

Sample Piano Voicings

Sample Bass

Sample Guitar Voicings (for chords with alterations)

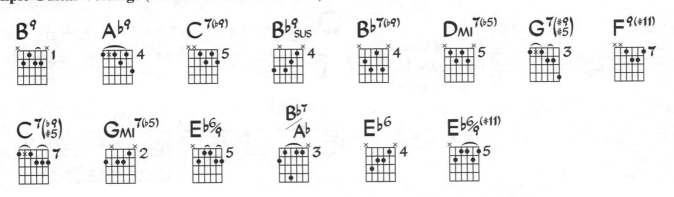

Smooth Samba

SUPPLEMENTAL MATERIAL - Smooth Samba

Scales for Soloing

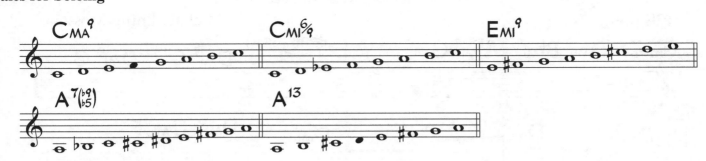

Sample Piano Voicings

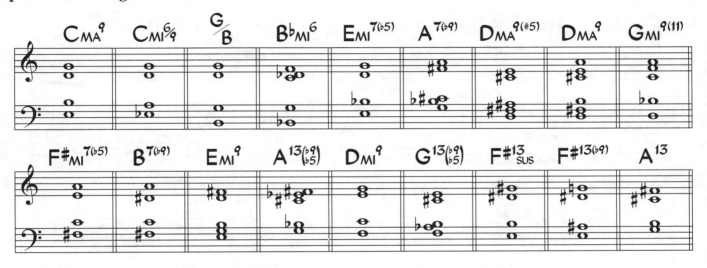

Sample Bass

Sample Guitar Voicings (for chords with alterations)

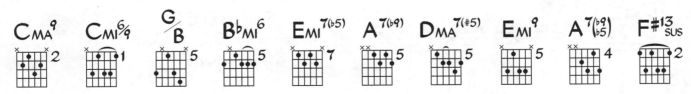

A Song For Horace

(dedicated to Horace Silver with deep respect)

Michael Philip Mossman

This part was originally written for trumpet.

SUPPLEMENTAL MATERIAL - A Song For Horace

Scales for Soloing

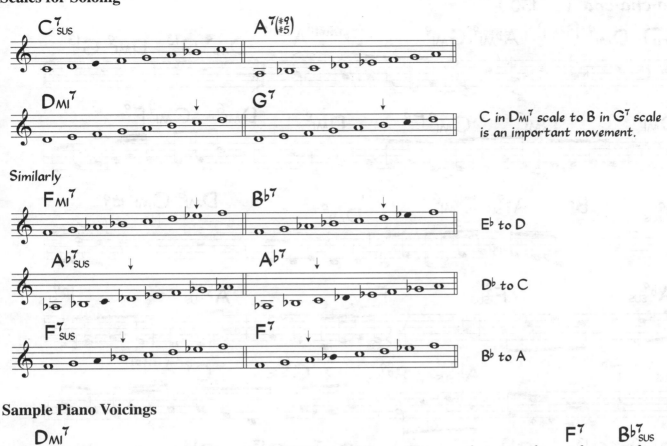

C in Dmi7 scale to B in G7 scale
is an important movement.

Similarly

Eb to D

Db to C

Bb to A

Sample Piano Voicings

A Song For Horace (harmony part)

This part was originally written for alto sax.

SUPPLEMENTAL MATERIAL - A Song For Horace

Scales for Soloing

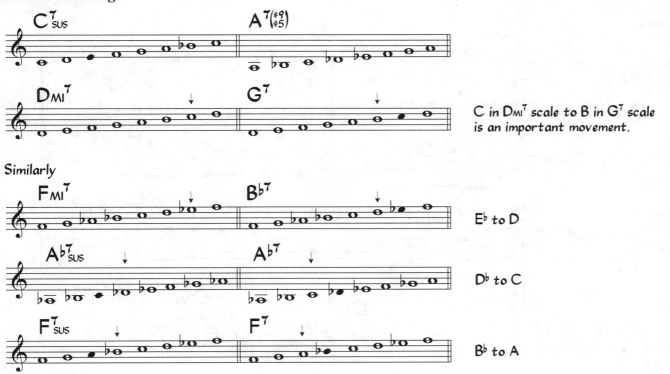

C in Dmi7 scale to B in G7 scale is an important movement.

Similarly

Eb to D

Db to C

Bb to A

Sample Guitar Voicings (for chords with alterations)

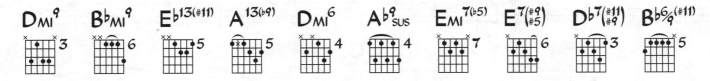

A Song For Horace (rhythm section)

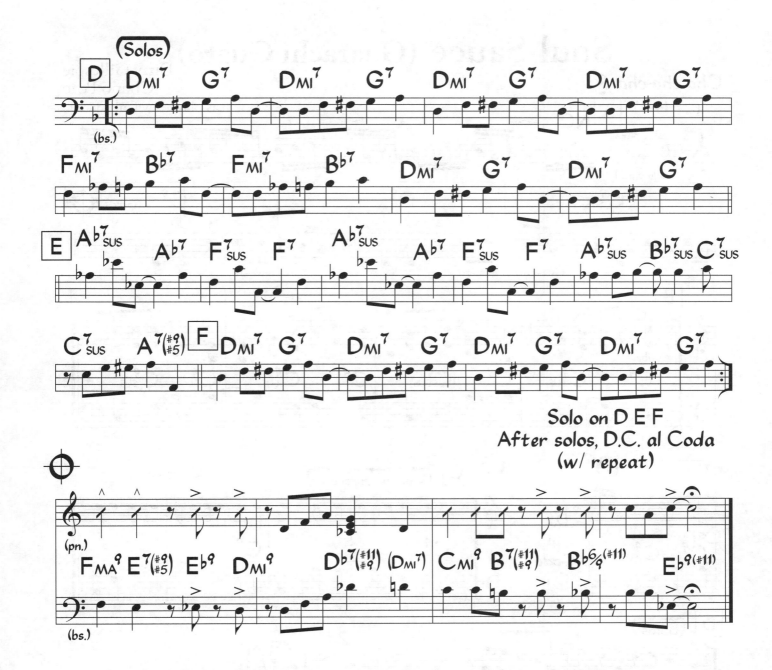

Solo on D E F
After solos, D.C. al Coda
(w/ repeat)

SUPPLEMENTAL MATERIAL - A Song For Horace

Sample Piano Voicings

Soul Sauce (Guarachi Guaro)

Dizzy Gillespie
Chano Pozo
(as played by Cal Tjader)

SUPPLEMENTAL MATERIAL - Soul Sauce

Scales for Soloing

Sample Piano Montuno

(both hands)

Sample Guitar Voicings (for chords with alterations)

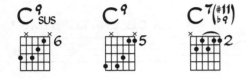

Tassajara

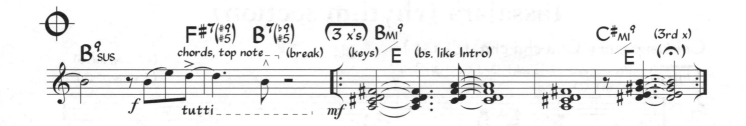

SUPPLEMENTAL MATERIAL - *Tassajara*

Scales for Soloing

Sample Piano Voicings

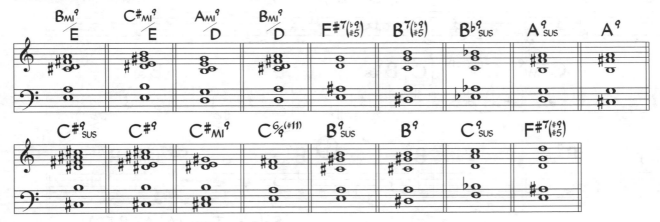

Sample Bass (for solos)

Letters B & C
similar to head

Tassajara (rhythm section)

SUPPLEMENTAL MATERIAL - *Tassajara*

Scales for Soloing (for chords with alterations)

Sample Piano Voicings

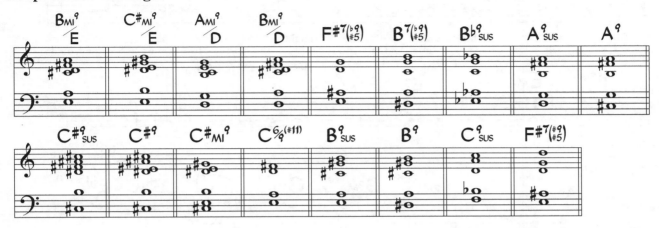

Sample Bass (for solos)

Letters B & C similar to head

Sample Guitar Voicings (for chords with alterations)

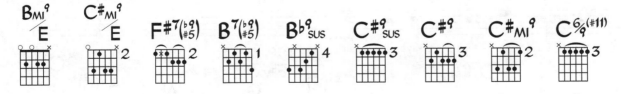

There's A Storm Inside

Music by
Chico Pinheiro
Lyric by Jesse Harris

Solo on A¹ A²,
play **B** as is,
vocal in at **C**
D.S. al Coda
(top lyric line)

250

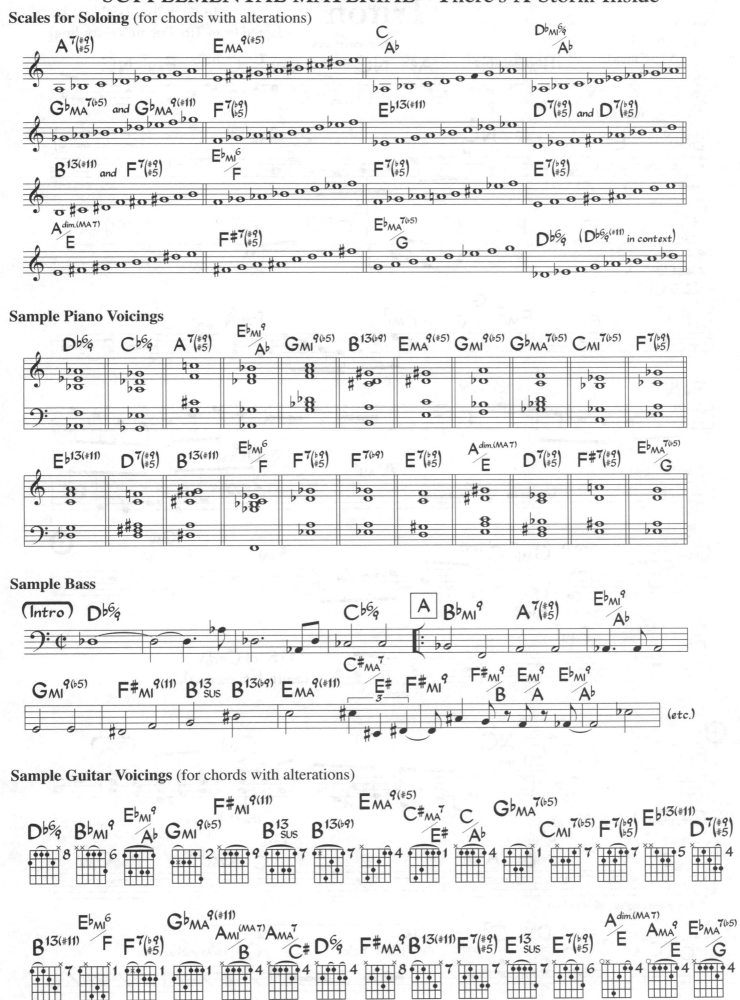

Triton

Jesús "Chucho" Valdés (adapted from Tito Puente's recording)

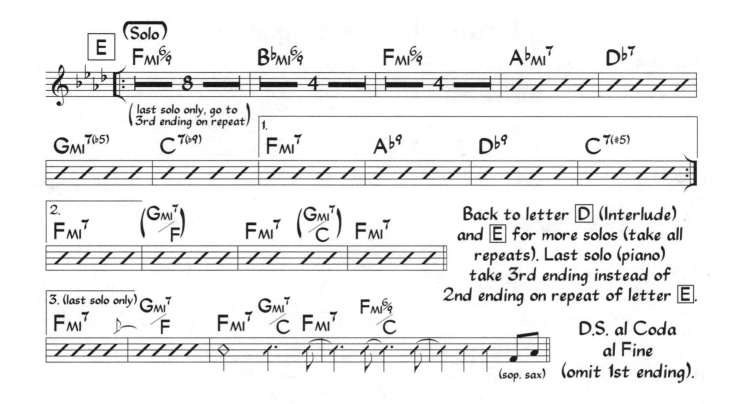

Back to letter [D] (Interlude) and [E] for more solos (take all repeats). Last solo (piano) take 3rd ending instead of 2nd ending on repeat of letter [E].

D.S. al Coda al Fine (omit 1st ending).

(sop. sax)

SUPPLEMENTAL MATERIAL - Triton

Scales for Soloing

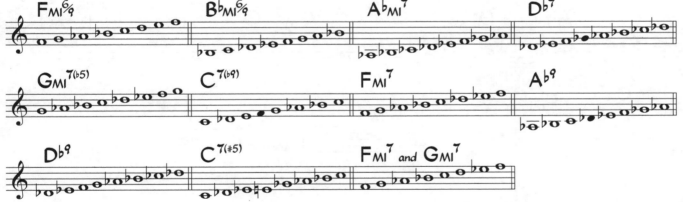

Sample Guitar Voicings (for chords with alterations)

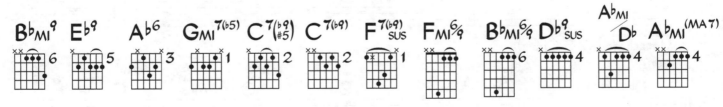

Triton (harmony parts)

Back to letter D (Interlude) and E for more solos (take all repeats). Last solo (piano) take 3rd ending instead of 2nd ending on repeat of letter E.

D.S. al Coda al Fine (omit 1st ending).

SUPPLEMENTAL MATERIAL - Triton

Scales for Soloing

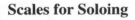

Sample Guitar Voicings (for chords with alterations)

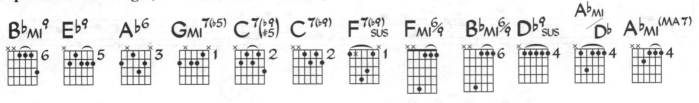

Triton (rhythm section)

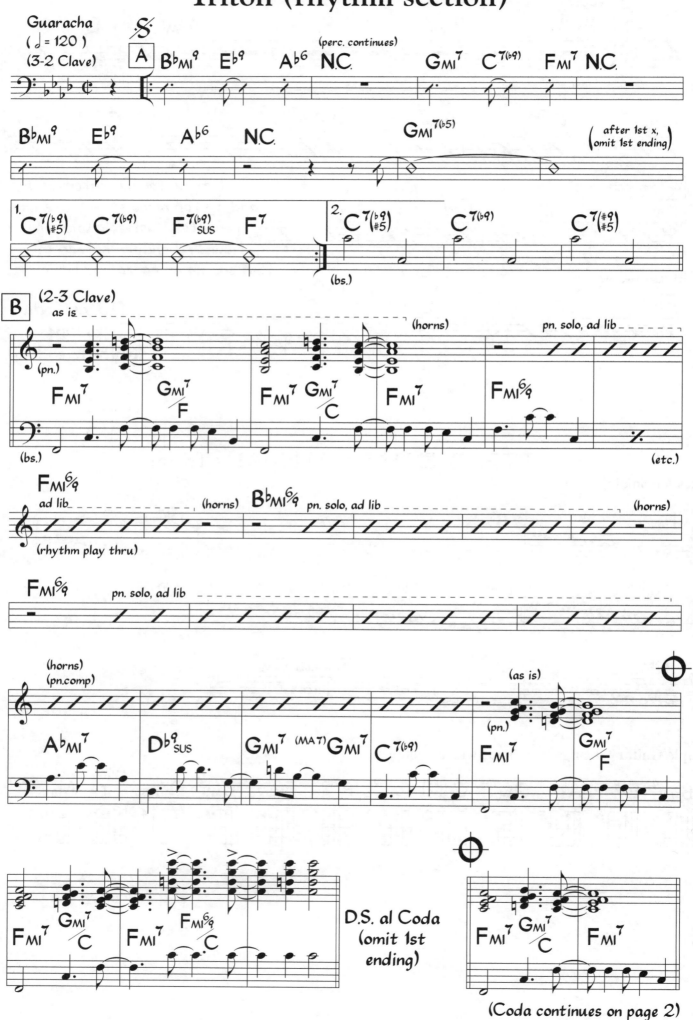

(Coda continues on page 2)

256

Solo on Tune,
(A¹ A² B¹ B² C¹ C²)
After solos, D.S. al Fine
(w/ repeats)

Scales for Soloing

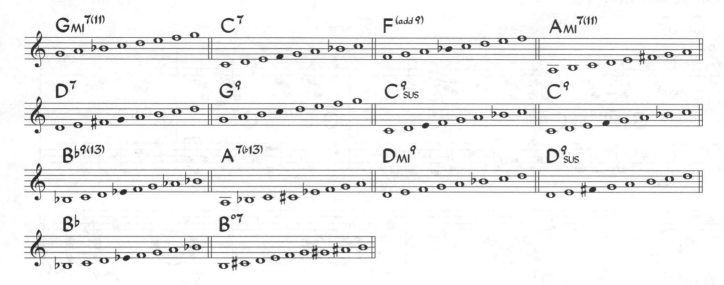

We Kinda Music (rhythm section)

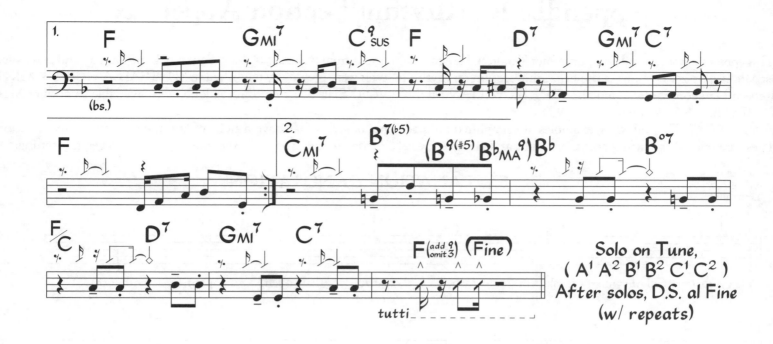

Solo on Tune,
(A¹ A² B¹ B² C¹ C²)
After solos, D.S. al Fine
(w/ repeats)

SUPPLEMENTAL MATERIAL - We Kinda Music

Scales for Soloing

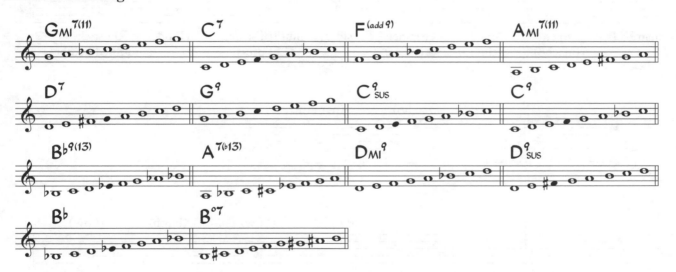

Sample Piano Voicings
(for chords with alterations)

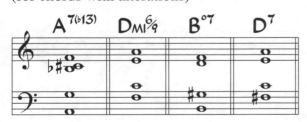

Sample Guitar Comping (sparse 16ths ad lib in Letter A)

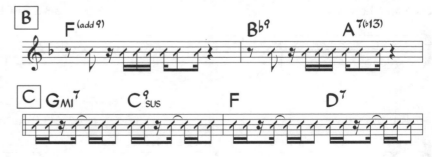

Sample Guitar Voicings (for chords with alterations)

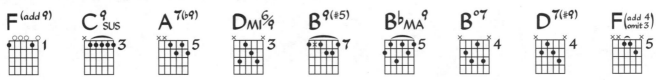

Appendix 1 - Rhythm Section Appendix

This appendix was transcibed by drummer Kendrick Freeman, with input from Rebeca Mauleón-Santana, Larry Dunlap and percussionist Michael Spiro. Portions of the beginning section on rhythmic styles were previously published in "THE SALSA GUIDEBOOK" by Rebeca Mauleón-Santana and also "THE BRAZILIAN MUSIC WORKSHOP" by Antonio Adolfo, both available from Sher Music Co., P.O.Box 445, Petaluma, CA 94953.

   NOTE: The following examples are simplified arrangements of styles that have a rich tradition, each with many variations. These are offered as starting points only, not as definitive "beats". Please see the "Sources" Appendix as a place to begin listening.

EXPLANATION OF NOTATION

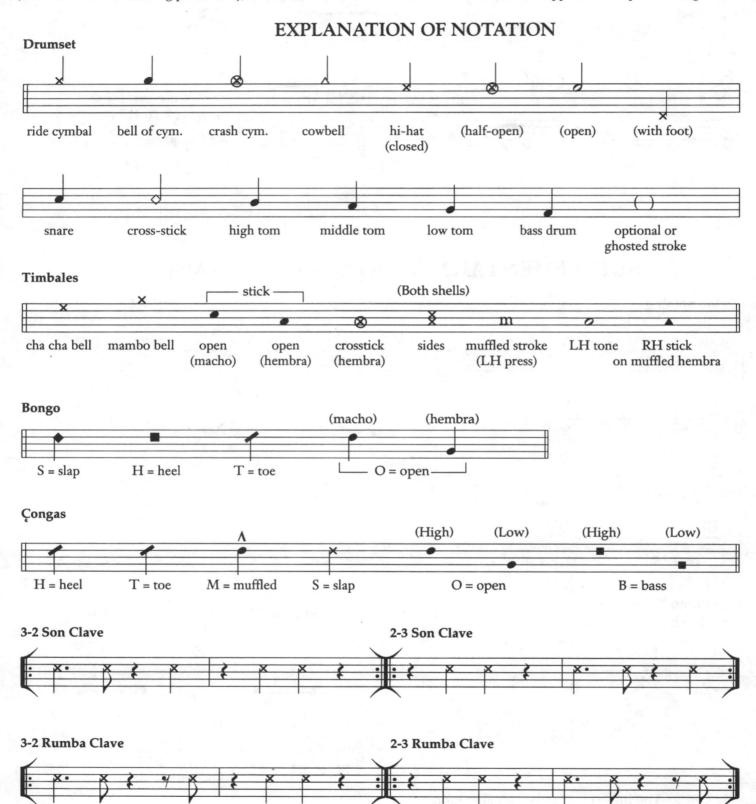

AFRO-CUBAN RHYTHMIC STYLES

Son Montuno
(2-3 Clave)

For the montuno/mambo sections of Son Montuno or Guaracha the percussionists switch to the patterns notated below as Mambo. (Bongo to Bongo bell. Cáscara to Mambo bell and Congas to two drums.)

Mambo/Guaracha
(2-3 Clave)

O = mouth of bell
• = neck of bell

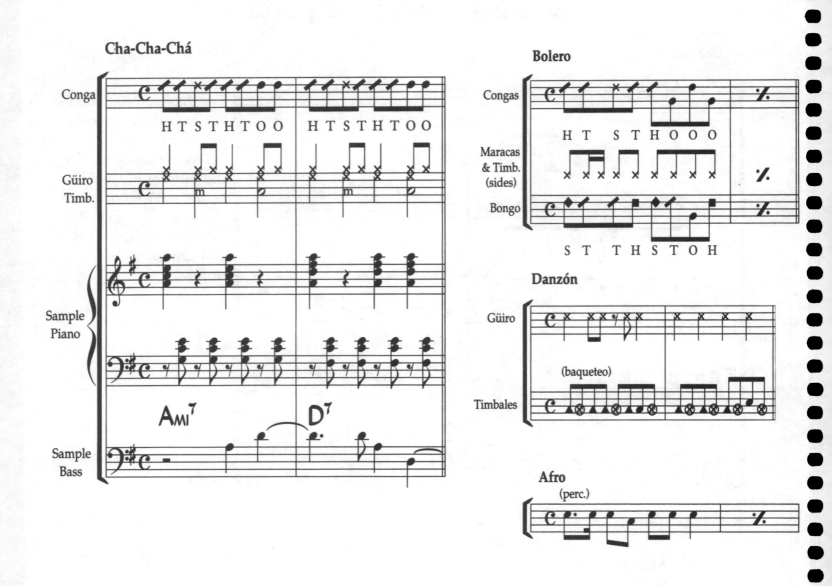

264

Conga Habanera   (Conga de Comparsa)

Bomba (Puerto Rico)

265

Guaguancó (ensemble)

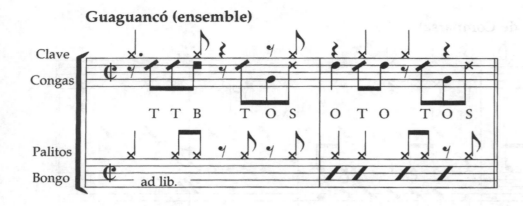

**Songo
(2-3 Rumba Clave)**

Plena (Puerto Rico)   (ensemble)

266

BRAZILIAN RHYTHMIC STYLES

Samba

Samba de Carnaval (Batucada)   (one of many possibilities)

Bossa Nova

DRUM &/OR PERCUSSION PARTS FOR INDIVIDUAL TUNES

Ao Vento

A D 16th Feel (Freely)

B E

Asa

(Djavan)

(Lee Ritenour)

Bananeira

A

B

Caballo Viejo

(woodblocks)   (guïro)   (bongo)

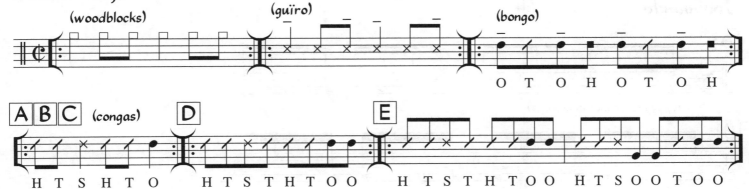

O T O H O T O H

A B C (congas)   D   E

H T S H T O   H T S T H T O O   H T S T H T O O   H T S O O T O O

269

Celeuma

(Intro)

A

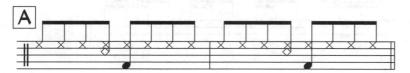

B

(w/ cross-stick variations)

Chakalaka

A

(Bass Solo)

Fuji

A

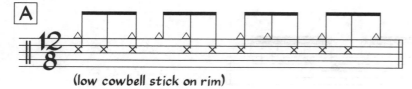

(low cowbell stick on rim)

Havana

Jobiniando

A

(w/ cross-stick variations)

B

La Cuna

Ladies In Mercedes

(Burton)

(ride pattern for solos is very free)

The Long Way Back

A

B

Lugar Comum

A

(bongo)

My Latin Brother

Double x

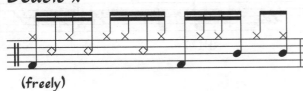

(freely)

Real Life

(drumset at measure 5)

(2nd x)

C

E

(omit 1st x)

Renata Maria

(shaker)

(woodblocks)

She Walks This Earth

(Chico C. version)

A

(tamborim)

B Samba

Tassajara

(Intro) A

(bass drum part)

B

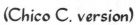

We Kinda Music

(Intro) A 16th Feel

2 (hi-hat continues)

(1st x only)

(B.D.)

APPENDIX II - MAKING USE OF SCALES WHEN IMPROVISING
by Larry Dunlap, Musical Editor

There are many (perhaps endless) approaches to improvising. My own early jazz education included almost no emphasis on scales. I learned chords first and was told to base most of my improvisation on chord tones. My personal (private) approach was to just play what sounded good to me.

Gradually I learned that non-chordal notes would sound great with various chords (6ths and 9ths with major 7th and dominant 7th chords, etc.). These were the extensions of the basic chords (and scale-based notes), but at the time I didn't think of these notes in this way. I just liked the way these non-chord tones sounded with the chords. I still remember when I first realized a 6th would sound good when played in a line over a 7th chord.

Of course, as my education progressed I became aware that certain scales were traditionally linked with certain chords. But I still remain more attracted to what sounds good with a chord, not generally thinking "This scale goes with this chord."

However, I do believe there is great value in recognizing the relationship between scales and chords. The following examples will give you a very basic knowledge of these relationships. Please explore these relationships further.

Many of the scales presented in this book include "avoid notes," portrayed as solid black notes among the open "white" notes. These are not notes to be strictly avoided. They are notes that will sound dissonant when held or stressed against the chord. If you want this dissonance, feel free to include these "avoid notes" in your improvised lines. In fact, I would expect to hear them within a solo.

Many of the most commonly used scales can be thought of as being based on a major scale, but beginning and ending on a different note of the scale. Here the names of some common chords and the scale commonly used with it.

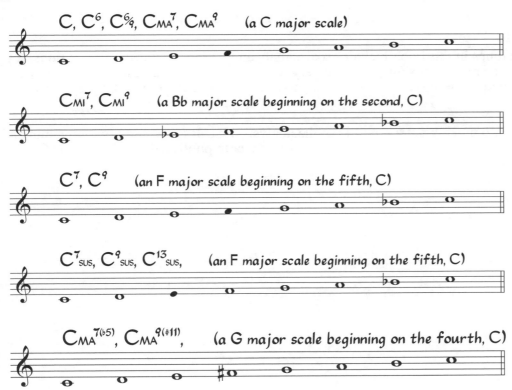

Other scales for other common chords:

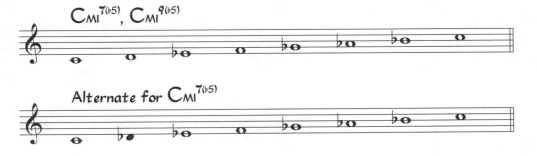

The Supplemental Material for each tunes in this book includes scales that can be used for the soloing sections. If there are many chords in the tune, space restrictions made it necessary to leave out the more basic scales. But they can be found here. Do not feel restricted to these scales. They are a good basis for starting out, but please always play what you think sounds best.

There are many publications that go into much greater detail in in the analysis of scales. I would highly recommend two books by Mark Levine, *The Jazz Theory Book* and *The Jazz Piano Book*, both published by Sher Music Co.. Above all, have fun and strive for tone.

APPENDIX III - GUITAR CHORD VOICINGS

Shown below are a sampling of some typical unaltered chord voicings which are not shown on page 2 of each tune. (Only altered guitar voicings are shown on page 2 of each tune.) Each voicing below should be moved up or down the guitar neck to make a different chord using the same voicing. For example, move the first voicing, Gma7, from the 3rd fret up to the 5th fret to make an Ama7.

Just a note on the altered guitar voicings on page 2 of each tune. For dominant 7(b9) chords, we usually used one of the three basic fingerings for diminished seventh chords (see the last 3 examples shown below). Also, depending on its position on the fingerboard, you'll find that the same augmented voicing can be used as a 7(#5) chord, a 9(#11) chord or a mi(ma7) chord. Lastly, the guitar voicings on page 2 of each tune may not always contain all the notes described by the chord symbol, e.g. the ninth may be omitted on a 9(#11) chord, the seventh omitted from a major nine chord, etc. (All guitar voicings were written by Ray Scott, veteran San Francisco guitarist and Stanford Jazz Workshop faculty member.)

Unaltered Guitar Voicings

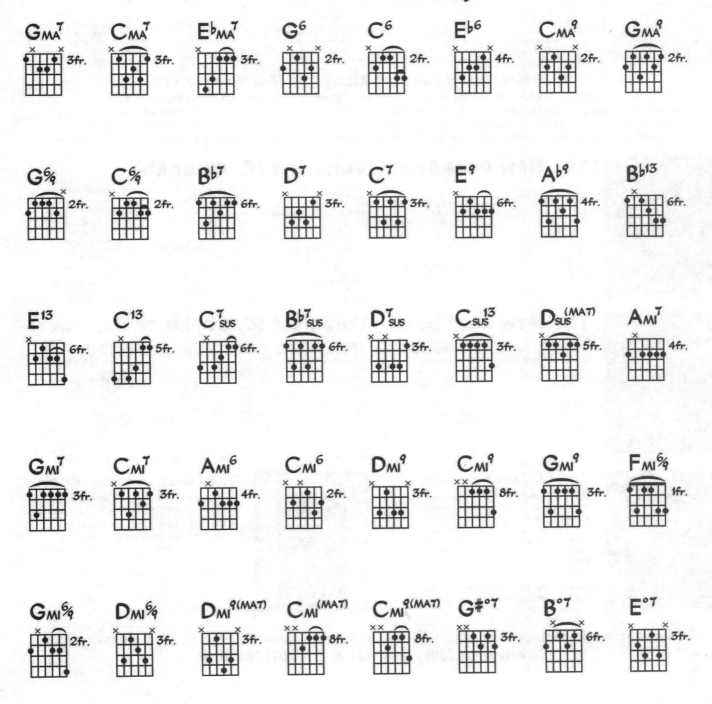

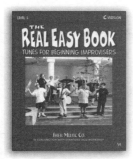

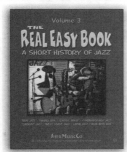

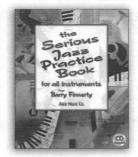

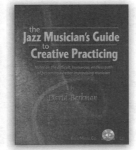

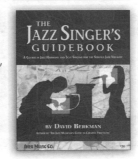

LATIN MUSIC BOOKS, CDs, DVD

The Latin Real Book (C, Bb or Eb)

The only professional-level Latin fake book ever published!
Over 570 pages. Detailed transcriptions exactly as recorded by:

Ray Barretto	Arsenio Rodriguez	Manny Oquendo	Ivan Lins
Eddie Palmieri	Tito Rodriguez	Puerto Rico All-Stars	Djavan
Fania All-Stars	Orquesta Aragon	Issac Delgaldo	Tom Jobim
Tito Puente	Beny Moré	Ft. Apache Band	Toninho Horta
Ruben Blades	Cal Tjader	Dave Valentin	Joao Bosco
Los Van Van	Andy Narell	Paquito D'Rivera	Milton Nascimento
NG La Banda	Mario Bauza	Clare Fischer	Leila Pinheiro
Irakere	Dizzy Gillespie	Chick Corea	Gal Costa
Celia Cruz	Mongo Santamaria	Sergio Mendes	And Many More!

The Latin Real Book Sampler CD

12 of the greatest Latin Real Book tunes as played by the original artists: Tito Puente, Ray Barretto, Andy Narell, Puerto Rico Allstars, Bacacoto, etc.

$16 list price. Available in U.S.A. only.

The Conga Drummer's Guidebook By Michael Spiro

Includes CD - $28 list price. The only method book specifically designed for the intermediate to advanced conga drummer. It goes behind the superficial licks and explains how to approach any Afro-Latin rhythm with the right feel, so you can create a groove like the pros!.

"This book is awesome. Michael is completely knowledgable about his subject."
– Dave Garibaldi

"A breakthrough book for all students of the conga drum."
– Karl Perazzo

Introduction to the Conga Drum - DVD By Michael Spiro

For beginners, or anyone needing a solid foundation in conga drum technique.

Jorge Alabe – "Mike Spiro is a great conga teacher. People can learn real conga technique from this DVD."

John Santos – "A great musician/teacher who's earned his stripes"

1 hour, 55 minutes running time. $25.

Muy Caliente!

Afro-Cuban Play-Along CD and Book
Rebeca Mauleón - Keyboard
Oscar Stagnaro - Bass
Orestes Vilató - Timbales
Carlos Caro - Bongos
Edgardo Cambon - Congas

Over 70 min. of smokin' Latin grooves!
Stereo separation so you can eliminate the bass or piano. Play-along with a rhythm section featuring some of the top Afro-Cuban musicians in the world! $18.

The True Cuban Bass

By Carlos Del Puerto, (bassist with Irakere) and Silvio Vergara, $22.

For acoustic or electric bass; English and Spanish text; Includes CDs of either historic Cuban recordings or Carlos playing each exercise; Many transcriptions of complete bass parts for tunes in different Cuban styles – the roots of Salsa.

101 Montunos By Rebeca Mauleón

The only comprehensive study of Latin piano playing ever published.

- Bi-lingual text (English/Spanish)
- 2 CDs of the author demonstrating each montuno
- Covers over 100 years of Afro-Cuban styles, including the danzón, guaracha, mambo, merengue and songo—from Peruchin to Eddie Palmieri. $28

The Salsa Guide Book By Rebeca Mauleón

The only complete method book on salsa ever published! 260 pages. $25.

Carlos Santana – "A true treasure of knowledge and information about Afro-Cuban music."
Mark Levine, author of The Jazz Piano Book. – "This is the book on salsa."
Sonny Bravo, pianist with Tito Puente – "This will be the salsa 'bible' for years to come."
Oscar Hernández, pianist with Rubén Blades – "An excellent and much needed resource."

The Brazilian Guitar Book By Nelson Faria, one of Brazil's best new guitarists.

- Over 140 pages of comping patterns, transcriptions and chord melodies for samba, bossa, baião, etc.
- Complete chord voicings written out for each example.
- Comes with a CD of Nelson playing each example.
- The most complete Brazilian guitar method ever published! $28.

Joe Diorio – "Nelson Faria's book is a welcome addition to the guitar literature. I'm sure those who work with this volume wiill benefit greatly"

Inside The Brazilian Rhythm Section By Nelson Faria and Cliff Korman

This is the first book/CD package ever published that provides an opportunity for bassists, guitarists, pianists and drummers to interact and play-along with a master Brazilian rhythm section. Perfect for practicing both accompanying and soloing.

$28 list price for book and 2 CDs - including the charts for the CD tracks and sample parts for each instrument, transcribed from the recording.

The Latin Bass Book
A PRACTICAL GUIDE By Oscar Stagnaro

The only comprehensive book ever published on how to play bass in authentic Afro-Cuban, Brazilian, Caribbean, Latin Jazz & South American styles. $34.

Over 250 pages of transcriptions of Oscar Stagnaro playing each exercise. Learn from the best!

Includes: 3 Play-Along CDs to accompany each exercise, featuring world-class rhythm sections.

Afro-Caribbean Grooves for Drumset

By Jean-Philippe Fanfant, drummer with Andy narell's band, Sakesho.

Covers grooves from 10 Caribbean nations, arranged for drumset.

Endorsed by Peter Erskine, Horacio Hernandez, etc.

CD includes both audio and video files. $25.

MORE JAZZ PUBLICATIONS

The Digital Real Book

On the web

Over 850 downloadable tunes from all the Sher Music Co. fakebooks.

See www.shermusic.com for details.

Foundation Exercises for Bass

By Chuck Sher

A creative approach for any style of music, any level, acoustic or electric bass. Perfect for bass teachers!

Filled with hundreds of exercises to help you master scales, chords, rhythms, hand positions, ear training, reading music, sample bass grooves, creating bass lines on common chord progressions, and much more.

$24

Jazz Guitar Voicings The Drop 2 Book

By Randy Vincent, Everything you need to know to create full chord melody voicings like Jim Hall, Joe Pass, etc. Luscious voicings for chord melody playing based on the "Drop 2" principle of chord voicings.

You will find that this book covers this essential material in a unique way unlike any other guitar book available.

Endorsed by Julian Lage, John Stowell, Larry Koonse, etc.

$25, includes 2 CDs.

Walking Bassics: The Fundamentals of Jazz Bass Playing

By swinging NY bassist Ed Fuqua

Includes transcriptions of every bass note on accompanying CD and step-by-step method for constructing solid walking bass lines. $22.

Endorsed by Eddie Gomez, Jimmy Haslip, John Goldsby, etc.

Three-Note Voicings and Beyond

By Randy Vincent, A complete guide to the construction and use of every kind of three-note voicing on guitar.

"Randy Vincent is an extraordinary musician. This book illuminates harmonies in the most sensible and transparent way." – **Pat Metheny**

"This book is full of essential information for jazz guitarists at any level. Wonderful!" – **Mike Stern**

194 pages, $28

Concepts for Bass Soloing

By Chuck Sher and Marc Johnson, (bassist with Bill Evans, etc.) The only book ever published that is specifically designed to improve your soloing! $26

- Includes two CDs of Marc Johnson soloing on each exercise
- Transcriptions of bass solos by: Eddie Gomez, John Patitucci, Scott LaFaro, Jimmy Haslip, etc.

"It's a pleasure to encounter a Bass Method so well conceived and executed." – **Steve Swallow**

The Jazz Piano Book

By Mark Levine, Concord recording artist and pianist with Cal Tjader. For beginning to advanced pianists. The only truly comprehensive method ever published! Over 300 pages. $32

Richie Beirach – "The best new method book available."
Hal Galper – "This is a must!"
Jamey Aebersold – "This is an invaluable resource for any pianist."
James Williams – "One of the most complete anthologies on jazz piano."

Also available in Spanish! ¡El Libro del Jazz Piano!

The Improvisor's Bass Method

By Chuck Sher. A complete method for electric or acoustic bass, plus transcribed solos and bass lines by Mingus, Jaco, Ron Carter, Scott LaFaro, Paul Jackson, Ray Brown, and more! Over 200 pages. $16

International Society of Bassists – "Undoubtedly the finest book of its kind."
Eddie Gomez – "Informative, readily comprehensible and highly imaginative"

The Blues Scales
ESSENTIAL TOOLS FOR JAZZ IMPROVISATION
By Dan Greenblatt

Great Transcriptions from Miles, Dizzy Gillespie, Lester Young, Oscar Peterson, Dave Sanborn, Michael Brecker and many more, showing how the Blues Scales are actually used in various styles of jazz.

Accompanying CD by author Dan Greenblatt and his swinging quartet of New York jazz musicians shows how each exercise should sound. And it also gives the student numerous play-along tracks to practice with. $22

Essential Grooves
FOR WRITING, PERFORMING AND PRODUCING CONTEMPORARY MUSIC
By 3 Berklee College professors: Dan Moretti, Matthew Nicholl and Oscar Stagnaro

- 41 different rhythm section grooves used in Soul, Rock, Motown, Funk, Hip-hop, Jazz, Afro-Cuban, Brazilian, music and more!
- Includes CD and multi-track DVD with audio files to create play-alongs, loops, original music, and more.

$24

Forward Motion
FROM BACH TO BEBOP
A Corrective Approach to Jazz Phrasing
By Hal Galper

- Perhaps the most important jazz book in a decade, Forward Motion shows the reader how to create jazz phrases that swing with authentic jazz feeling.
- Hal Galper was pianist with Cannonball Adderley, Phil Woods, Stan Getz, Chet Baker, John Scofield, and many other jazz legends.
- Each exercise available on an interactive website so that the reader can change tempos, loop the exercises, transpose them, etc. $30.

The World's Greatest Fake Book

Jazz & Fusion Tunes by: **Coltrane, Mingus, Jaco, Chick Corea, Bird, Herbie Hancock, Bill Evans, McCoy, Beirach, Ornette, Wayne Shorter, Zawinul, AND MANY MORE!** $32

Chick Corea – "Great for any students of jazz.'
Dave Liebman – "The fake book of the 80's."
George Cables – "The most carefully conceived fake book I've ever seen."